Life with Bluebell

This book is dedicated with love to the three men still at home – my husband Derek and our two younger sons, Daniel and Simon, who have at times nearly been moved to eating their meals wearing wellington boots to ward off badger and fox cubs from playing with their feet. They have taken over doing feeds when I have been away and are always willing to help when one pair of hands is not enough. My sincere appreciation for all you have done.

Life with Bluebell

and Other Tales from an Animal Orphanage

Pauline Kidner

BCA

LONDON   NEW YORK   SYDNEY   TORONTO

This edition published 1993
by BCA, by arrangement with
Robinson Publishing Ltd

CN 5703

Typeset by Hewer Text Composition Services, Edinburgh
Printed in Great Britain by Redwood Books, Trowbridge, Wiltshire

Contents

Foreword

There are many people who may think that looking after orphaned and injured wild animals is a bit of a breeze. After all, what do you have to do all day apart from give them food and water? Anyone who holds this view will, after reading this book, think again. It takes enormous stamina, care, commitment, humour and love to devote our life to such a task. Pauline and Derek Kidner possess all of these qualities and more.

We first met when I wanted to film a young badger searching for grubs in a hollow log, and heard about Bluebell, an orphaned cub who was being reared by the Kidners on the farm in Somerset. A phone call and a day or two later, I had converted one of the farm outbuildings into a replica of a deciduous woodland, and was lying on the floor with a very inquisitive badger investigating the contents of my ears. Throughout the filming, Pauline was dashing to and fro, mucking out the foxes and mink, feeding the squirrels and the tortoise and the pigs and the chickens and . . . still managing to offer us cups of coffee with home-made biscuits in her usual calm and friendly manner, as if such a whirlwind of activity were the norm.

Since then, I have been helped by Derek and Pauline on many occasions, and I know now that this gruelling schedule really is the norm for them both, and that only people with such an affinity with animals could possibly hope to remain cheery throughout it all. And perhaps this is the secret. It seems to me that it is a dry and consistent sense of humour, a facet of Pauline's personality which finds its way into almost every element of her life, that sees her through the highlights, and the tragedies of caring for those creatures whose misfortune in the wild brings them the good fortune of coming into her care. If I were an orphaned badger or a roe deer with a broken leg, I cannot think of anywhere I would rather be.

All the requirements for food, veterinary care, heating and enclosures for the many creatures which are passed on to Pauline take a heavy financial toll. Much of the work that goes on at New Road Farm does so behind closed doors and is funded entirely by monies raised by the farm itself. Unfortunately this is not sufficient to support the ever growing number of casualties which find their way there, and the budgetary strain is close to bursting point. But the tenacious spirit which motivates Pauline has led to the creation of the Bluebell Set. By joining this animal welfare society you are making a personal statement that you too care for the wellbeing of our wild creatures and, into the deal, you can benefit from a host of special privileges at New Road Farm. Details of how to join the set can be found in the back of this book.

Simon King

Simon King has been making wildlife films for over 13 years, including 'Walk on the Wild Side' for BBC1, and 'Tracks' for BBC2. He also worked on 'Trials of Life' for BBC1. His book Simon King's Wild Guide, *on how to watch wild animals in Britain, was published in 1994.*

1

New Road Farm:
How It All Started

> Housekeeper required for farmer and three children
> on a small dairy farm. Driver an advantage. Apply
> Box No. 418.

This advertisement was the reason I was driving on a dark
November evening in 1977 through deepest Somerset. We
had spoken on the phone and I had arranged to meet the farmer
and his children the following day. My own marriage had broken
up and, living temporarily with my parents, I was looking for a
way of supporting my two-year-old son and six-year-old red setter.
Farming was not new to me; I had worked as a dairymaid for two
years after leaving school and had thoroughly enjoyed milking a
herd of Jersey and Guernsey cows and looking after a deep-litter
unit of laying poultry. Funnily enough, both my sister and I worked
on farms after leaving school – fairly unusual for the daughters of
a policeman with no rural upbringing or background!

Turning into the gateway of a very old farmhouse, the headlights
showed a puddled yard. A scruffy Jack Russell barked at the
intrusion, and a light shone out from the backhouse door as
Derek came forward to meet me. I took to him immediately. He
was tall with light brown hair, his bearded face softened by smiling
eyes. Scooping the dog up into my arms, I went into the farmhouse

kitchen where an old Rayburn radiated warmth. (I was yet to find out that this was the *only* warm room in the eight-bedroomed house.) The children were busy playing a board game in the sitting room, in front of a roaring log fire. Derek and I sat in the kitchen and, over a cup of coffee, he explained the situation. His wife had left him for someone else and, with a farm and three children aged four, seven and eight to organize, he desperately needed help. The family had only lived at the farm for six months; before that it had been the home of Derek's parents, who had moved to a smaller house nearby. Warned that I would need to keep my coat on (!), I was taken on a tour of the rest of the house, many rooms of which were not in use. I suppose most normal people would have been completely put off by the crumbling plaster and peeling wallpaper, but I am blessed with a vivid imagination and a love of DIY, so my mind was running riot. So many little things could be done that would make the place more homely – especially a lampshade to cover the bare light bulb in the kitchen! And I did think that Derek was rather nice. (He told me later that he thought the same about me because I picked up the dog, even though I was wearing a smart cream coat.)

We chatted for a while longer in the kitchen, both of us laughing at a couple of misunderstandings that had arisen from our previous conversation. I had to explain that my auburn-haired responsibility was a red setter and not another child, and Derek, upon my asking 'What about references?', had said he could probably get one, when I had really meant did he require one from me? Surprisingly quickly it was arranged that I should move in the following week, and we both crossed our fingers that the children and dogs would all agree.

From the moment that we moved in (complete with lampshade) time seemed to fly. My son Simon got on well with Derek's younger son Daniel, aged four, though they were complete opposites and remain so to this day. Kelly and Barry, with just one year between them, were typical brother and sister – they loved to hate each other, but if you dared to say anything against one, the other one would instantly stick up for them. Sheena, the red setter, thought Chutney, the Jack Russell, was great fun and vice versa, so both the children and the dogs did agree (most of the time), and as Derek and I felt as if we had known each other for years, we soon became a family.

Derek and I had so much in common. We both loved the farm

and enjoyed working with the animals. We had been attracted to each other right from the start, enjoying each other's company, and as we had both experienced broken marriages, valued having a partner who was also a friend. It was not long before we were living as a married couple (it was also a very cold house!) but some years passed before we actually married in 1981. On talking to the children much later, I discovered that my arrival had made two great changes in their lives – one was the use of hot water bottles and the other was the introduction of peanut butter to their diet, and both were much approved of!

Christmas was drawing nearer and the excitement of sorting out presents and preparing all the traditional things was an extra bonus to our new lives. Paper chains, making decorations, dressing the Christmas tree, besides filling four stockings and buying the presents – there was so much to do in such a short time. This was the first Christmas that Derek's parents had not lived at the farm and in past years Derek's sister Rosemary and her family, as well as Derek's family, had all come for lunch in the farmhouse, so we decided to continue with tradition and have done so every Christmas since.

Mr and Mrs Kidner were very much country people, leading quiet lives, having always earned their living from the land, and a more gentle couple one could never wish to meet. From the time of our coming to the farm, Simon and I were treated as grandson and daughter. Mr Kidner was in partnership with Derek, but from this time on his health started to fail and he slowly became less able to do so much on the farm. He was firmly convinced that I was 'all right' after finding me plaiting onions – obviously a country craft well respected! The Kidner name originated from this area and we can be pretty sure that anyone with the same name is a relation, one way or another. The family is quite large, although one branch moved away to Norfolk; now, after many years married to Derek, I still come across people who are related to me.

Christmas was followed by one of the heaviest New Year snow falls for several years. Our own road was completely closed for two days, and even after that could only be safely tackled by tractor. This part of the Somerset Levels looks even more beautiful blanketed in white, icicles draping the spindly arms of the withy (willow) trees that stand like sentries on the banks of the waterways, known locally as rhines, that divide our fields. There were drifts of snow up to five and six feet high in certain parts and it was great for tobogganing and building snowmen. Trying to keep these lovely thoughts in mind was not always easy when wearing one's overcoat upstairs making the beds, or sitting in front of a roaring log fire with so many draughts that I swear at times I felt my nose and feet were suffering from frost bite. Even more so when the snow gave way to the thaw – anyone who has lived in an old house with lead piping will know exactly the outcome. It is on these occasions, whilst paddling in several inches of water, that one must remind oneself how lucky one is that the floor is flagstoned and will be so easy to mop up!

The farm cat, Susie (who turned out to be a boy named Sue) had never been allowed into the house, and if she had ever dared would quickly have been shouted at and even given some assistance in leaving. The extra-cold weather now drew her to the warmth coming from the kitchen, and Simon, always used to animals being allowed in the house, could not understand why she would not come right in. When you are only two years old, picking up a large cat can be quite difficult, so Simon usually ended up with the top half of the cat in his arms and the remainder dragging behind; then he would triumphantly deposit the cat close to the Rayburn where, to start with, it remained with a haunted look of terror, waiting for the eviction order. Needless to say, it did not take long for it to realize that the house rules had changed, and Susie was soon an almost permanent fixture as a tabby rug in the kitchen. We even managed to convince Derek that, with the amount of rats and mice that there must be on the farm, we could do with a couple more kittens, purely on the understanding that they would remain outside cats. (Obviously they did so – until the following winter. Well, cats aren't silly, are they?) So Blackie, obviously all black, and Becky, a pretty tortoiseshell, joined the fold. Blackie became Derek's favourite and one of the few animals whose death nearly moved him to tears. Becky, a dear little cat, was with us for many years.

Spring unfolded a fresh new year, and many plants in the garden started to push through their new shoots. I had not realized some of them were even there. The farm has a large, partially walled garden with the twin disadvantages of having clay soil and facing east; there was also a large vegetable garden which we no longer have. I thoroughly enjoyed the freedom of being outside and slowly became more involved with helping on the farm, especially as Mr Kidner's involvement became less and less. Much of the garden had been put to grass to make it easier to manage and I spent a lot of time creating flower beds and tidying up. Barry, Derek's eldest boy, was quite disgusted with all these flower beds – 'and was it ever necessary' – a chip off the old (Grandad Kidner's) block. Mr Kidner was a great believer in cutting down and cutting off. Mrs Kidner had a beautiful laburnum tree in the garden until Mr Kidner decided it was too tall: it was immediately cut down and never flowered again!

With warmer days we felt more inclined to work in the evenings, so decorating was started in the house and small alterations were made. Derek began to dread the sentence that starts with 'I've been thinking . . .', and still does to this day because he says it always means work. What's the point of having a decent chicken house, which only needs a lick of creosote, unless we get some hens and have some free-range chickens? Twelve brown hens were soon in residence and I came to love the way they look, as though they gather their petticoats to run towards you, when you have some food. This was an idea that turned into quite a hobby.

It is amazing just how many breeds of poultry there are. Many are frequently advertised in our local paper and, once we started to collect them, the varieties came to seem endless. Frizzles with all their feathers turning backwards, Polish with large pom-poms on the back of their heads, Silkies which are nearly all fluff with feathers only on their wings; every time we went to buy a pair, we usually saw some other breeds that we liked. Over the next few years our collection grew until we had over forty different breeds of poultry, from chickens to geese to peafowl and ducks.

The first pair of peafowl that we acquired came from a local farmer, and it was the first time that Derek had ever encountered such large birds. Armed with sacks to put them in, he thought that the farmer would show him how to catch them. It's quite important with an adult pair not to catch the male bird by his tail, or else you end up paying for a peacock whose long train is no longer attached to the bird but is left grasped in your hand. 'No trouble at all in catching them', said the old farmer, with his weathered face, as he led us down a muddy lane. 'Them's shut in an old chicken house.' True to his word, he took us to an old 6-foot by 4-foot ark. Mistakenly believing that the farmer was being polite in allowing him in through the door first, Derek soon found the door hurriedly shut behind him followed by a short verbal lesson on 'how to do it'. The shrieking of the peafowl had to be heard to be believed, and soon clouds of dust were drifting from every gap of the well-worn house. Indeed it was incredible, with all the commotion, that the walls remained intact. Not to be beaten, Derek emerged triumphantly with two peafowl in the bag. The fact that he looked slightly dishevelled and could have auditioned for the Black and White Minstrel Show was neither here nor there!

Part of the fun in collecting poultry was not just the travelling to different locations to buy them but also the characters that we met at each new place. We learnt so much more about poultry, diseases and breeding than you could ever pick up from a book. This is something I have found all the way through. People who have spent their lives studying a particular breed of animals are always willing to offer help and advice when asked and will impart knowledge that has taken them years to acquire. (Little things, such as when you have peacocks, the race is on in the spring as to who can get to the cauliflowers first, and flower beds full of wallflowers becoming rows of stalks, these are things that you find out for yourself!)

As the stock increased, you can imagine the problems that arose when it came to holiday time. My own parents, living not very far away, were always keen gardeners and Dad was a good handyman, so they often came over to the farm and would help in any way that they could. Innocently offering to look after the place while we were on holiday in 1980, they were not quite aware of what they were taking on. At this time, with all the different breeds of poultry, there were twenty-seven different chicken houses that needed to be shut up at night; and what's more, animals get used to a certain routine, and changing it can really upset the apple cart. So: 'Walk geese through the orchard into house number fifteen before putting ducks into house number seven as geese will chase them. Crested ducks go in house number six but look out for Sid (brown duck with lop-sided pom-pom) as he will chase others out if he goes in first . . .' Four sheets of A4 paper with written instructions, colour-coded routes and numbered chicken houses were left to 'make things easier'. It's a wonder my mother was not grey by the time we came home.

Just prior to leaving it was discovered that two Muscovy ducks had gone broody in the cider house. One was slightly at risk to the fox, sitting as she was behind a large tractor tyre, and the other was up in the loft. Both were sitting on eighteen eggs and we were not sure how long they had been broody, so we just had to hope they would be all right until we came back. We showed Mum where the one was in the cider house but told her not to worry about the one in the loft as she would come out each day to get her food and water. A car packed with luggage and excited children waving goodbye left the farmyard, with both my parents putting on a brave face: someone was coming in to do the milking but they were going to have plenty to do with all the odds and ends.

When we had arrived safely and had unpacked, I waited until the evening to ring and check that all was well. A flustered Mother answered the phone – yes, they had managed the shutting up all right . . . they may not be in the right houses but *everything* has been put away for the night! Reading between the lines, I had a mental picture of the two of them coursing the orchard with huge butterfly nets catching everything on two legs. Mother did assure me that it got easier each day as they got into a routine. The most harrowing part for her was when one Muscovy duck proudly produced eighteen bright yellow ducklings on the fourth day of our holiday – she did not tell me when I rang in case I worried. Dutifully returning to the nest behind the tyre each night, Mum was vexed when the next day there were only fifteen ducklings; the numbers went down each day until, by the time we arrived home, there were only nine left. She was sure it was her fault – maybe she should have shut them up or looked after them better. We assured her that it was just one of those things. However, on checking the other Muscovy duck in the loft, we found that she also had hatched her eighteen eggs – yet she was brooding not eighteen ducklings but twenty-seven! So she had been stealing them from the duck below, but just how she got them up into the loft we will never know.

Although our many poultry were bringing in a small income, the farm was finding it increasingly difficult to support two families. This was at the time when the government was encouraging farmers to increase milk production with the hopes of Britain becoming self-sufficient in dairy products. Grants were being offered to small farmers to increase their herds and therefore the milk yield. Derek contacted the local agricultural advisory group, and after lengthy discussions decided to take up bank loans to improve our buildings and eventually increase our herd of Friesians from thirty-five to sixty. This was a four-year grading-up scheme with the government. Though it would mean a lot more work, we went ahead as by this time we were both committed to the farm and could see no other way forward. Derek did a lot of the building work himself or helped when contractors were called in, and this was all additional work to the general running of the farm.

Winter had come around again, meaning extra work with all the animals indoors for feeding and cleaning – and isn't it always at these times when things go wrong? We always reckoned that the animals get into a huddle every so often to decide who is going to fall ill or die just when we are ready to go out. It was a Friday afternoon and Derek had just finished the milking. A young heifer due to calve had been brought in with the herd to get used to the routine before she calved down. Finding the gate open by the yard, she wandered up by the haybarn. Derek called me to help turn her back into the yard; by the time we had returned she had decided to walk along a narrow path between the hay and a four-foot stone wall, at the back of the haybarn, that led to the slurry pit. Worried that she would fall in, Derek jumped over the stone wall and waved his arms to make her turn back, away from the danger of the slurry pit. As she did not have enough room to turn around, he was expecting her to walk backwards into the open again. I kept back and watched as there was nothing I could do at that particular time, and the fewer people around to distract her the better. She, unfortunately, was quite adamant that forward she wanted to go, irrespective of this man shouting and jumping up and down. In horror I watched as she made a rush at him; I saw Derek fall backwards and disappear from view, and the wall physically moving as she pushed past him. This was followed by a silence that seemed an eternity. Running forward, I saw Derek heave himself up; it was obvious that he had injured his shoulder. Staggering out to catch his breath, he watched as the heifer did a neat U-turn at the end of the haybarn and returned back down the path, almost as if to inspect the damage. Chasing her down to the yard, my next actions were to bundle Derek into the car and off to hospital to find out exactly what injuries had been caused.

On arrival at casualty, we found the usual queue and so searched for a coffee machine and waited our turn. When we did eventually see the doctor, he turned out to be an Oriental gentleman who as yet had not completely mastered the English language; so we had great difficulty in explaining exactly how the accident had occurred. On returning from X-ray, our confidence in him floundered a little bit more when we found both him and the nurse scrutinizing the X-ray and comparing it with a photograph in a book – which we could only assume to have been of a healthy shoulder (we hoped). Still not quite sure whether in fact the collar-bone had been broken, the doctor decided it was best to put the arm in a sling and for Derek to return on the Monday to see a consultant who could indeed confirm if there had been a fracture.

When your right arm is out of action, you soon realize how little you can do with just one arm. Eating, dressing, washing all become a work of art. It was like having a baby again, having to cut Derek's food up for him and catching him when he nearly fell over trying to get his trousers on. Had it not been for the pain he was in, it could have been quite amusing. Even the natural action requiring toilet paper can have its difficulties.

Returning to the hospital on the Monday, Derek went in to see the specialist on his own. Much to my surprise, he returned minus the sling having been told that it was not in fact broken but just badly bruised. But what about all the pain he had been getting during the weekend? 'Ah!', explained the consultant, 'it would have been better if you had not kept the arm restricted and had exercised the arm to ease the bruising.'

For those who may think that Derek is the only accident-prone person on the farm, I must add that I have been seen riding backwards, bareback, on a very large pig going at what seemed to me to be at least 30 to 40 miles an hour, with a very worried look on my face. A sow that we had been trying to move ran straight through my legs instead of going around me, lifting me completely helpless on to her back. How Derek managed to keep a straight face I will never know and, to my great relief, there was no one around with a camera. That would have been one photograph that would have been endlessly passed around.

One person who would really have liked to take a photograph is my friend Sheena. We have known each other for many years and take great delight in reminding each other of the stupid things we have done in the past. We first met when we were both receptionists in a hotel and, in later years, we ran a pub together. It is one of those friendships that no matter how long it is since we last saw each other, we are on close terms straight away. (I dare not tell the story of why my red setter was named after her – that will have to wait for another day.) Sheena has stayed in the hotel trade and is now a conference co-ordinator. She frequently stays at the farm and, not being a country girl herself, has in times of crisis helped out but not always willingly. One weekend found her pulling on the end of a rope with the rest of us helping to calve a cow. (She had her eyes closed, of course.) It was as close to nature as she had ever been, and she certainly did not want to get any closer. *Next* time, if she really had to help, she was going to be up the other end, holding her hand – or paw – or whatever it's called.

On another occasion, we were checking the sheep as we wandered back from a walk and found one caught up in the brambles. It was one of the Jacob sheep which are usually easier to handle because of their horns. It gives you something to grasp in addition to their actual fleece. As we pulled it out of the hedge, it had several briars still trapped in its fleece. 'You hold on to its horns,' I told Sheena, 'then I can pull the briars off.' When you have been used to handling animals, it appears easier than it is and I never really gave it much thought. Changing over positions, with Sheena grasping the horns with all her might, the sheep sensed that the restraint was only on its horns and not on its body as before, and decided to make a break for it. Size for size, there was not much in it as Sheena does not make much impression over five foot; but her wet wellingtons in the thick November grass were making skid marks rather than finding any suitable footing. It is very difficult to offer advice of any kind when laughing, but I was very impressed with the way she was anchoring and managing to slow the sheep down, by not only digging her heels in the ground but dragging her bottom as well. I think really the sheep tired first, but Sheena reckoned she finally had it under control. Concealing my mirth, I tried not to say too much but the saying 'looking like you've been dragged through a hedge backwards' was running through my mind.

The briars came away without too much trouble but worse was to come. Mustering a second breath, the sheep twisted its head: and using all its strength, it shot away leaving Sheena with one horn still grasped tightly in her hand. The face that had been flushed pink from the race quickly drained and her legs gave out from under her. The sheep, now free of the briars and those silly people, started to graze, completely oblivious of the horn that was missing; it watched as the two figures made their way back to the farmhouse, one supporting the other who appeared to have rubber legs, to get some coffee and maybe a brandy too!

For Sheena, the enjoyable part of coming to stay was going down to the local with Derek and meeting the village characters. In the days when cheese was made on the farm, a lot of cider was made also and men would work for a few hours and in return would have some cider. Those who could still get around on bikes would often call in to have a chat and cadge a glass of cider. There was no cider made at our farm by then, but Derek's Uncle Joe still had some on his farm and often the old cronies would meet up and recall the old days over a few jars. Uncle Joe was a bachelor and nothing had changed on his farm for years. Derek had some cattle grazing down there, and he took Sheena with him to check on them and meet Uncle Joe. He was busy mending a fence when they arrived but was happy to stop and talk, to ask after the family and how the stock was. Two of his friends turned up as they were talking so the offer of a glass of cider was soon made, and they drifted back to the barn where it was stored. The apple boxes were pulled

. . . leaving Sheena with one horn still grasped tightly in her hand.

11

out so that they could sit in the sun, and the usual banter of who had made the best hay or had the biggest animals went on between them all. The cider glasses were always stacked on the same shelf in the barn but were not always washed; however, realizing there was a lady amongst them, one of the old chaps duly spat on his dirty old handkerchief and shone one of the glasses especially for Sheena. (She remarked afterwards that she hadn't been very bothered as the cider was strong enough to kill all known germs anyway!)

There then followed an enjoyable couple of hours listening to all their stories, including the one about when they returned fairly drunk after a skittles match one evening to a farmer friend's house, and brought a cockerel into the kitchen for a mock auction – until the poor man's wife got out of bed and put an end to all the commotion! A giggly pair returned from checking the cattle. So Sheena must enjoy her visits because she keeps coming back.

Tragically, the following year Uncle Joe was killed in a farm accident. He was always rather wary of driving the tractor anyway, but on this day he hitched a tow-rope too high on the tractor to move a large tree stump. The tractor turned over on top of him and he was crushed. It seemed such a waste. So well known by many locals, he was sorely missed and another link with the old days was lost for ever. It is these incidents that make you aware of the dangers of the machinery used every day on the farm, especially when there are children around.

By continuing the scheme with the government, we were keeping all our female calves so that they would eventually join the herd once they were old enough to calve themselves – usually a period of at least three years. This meant that the feed bills were high, with still only the small herd bringing in any revenue from milk. Hence the bank balance was not looking very healthy, thanks also to the bank interest rates which at that time absolutely rocketed.

It was becoming increasingly more difficult to manage with so little money, and the workload was increasing as we were keeping larger numbers of animals. Derek's father, due to illness, was by now unable to do any work on the farm. It kept both of us working very long days.

The sense of humour that we share and our understanding of each other have helped in times of working extremely closely with each other under pressure. There was just no spare cash to be able to employ anyone to help with the workload. Luckily, the government brought out the Youth Opportunity Scheme at that time, and we were able to employ a young lad. This worked very well. Kevin was with us for six months and it was great to have an extra pair of hands around. We had several lads and one girl over a period of time and it worked well for both sides: they had the opportunity to gain experience in farming, and we were able to have some help on a wage that we could afford to pay. All of them left to go into permanent jobs which was basically the aim of the scheme.

If there was one thing that Kevin liked to do it was dig holes! Great if something died because you could give him a spade, point him in the right direction and he was as happy as a sand boy for the next couple of hours. Not so good when getting him to help in the garden. Our potato and runner bean crops were complete failures that year due to the weeks (even months) that we had to wait for them to come through, as he had dug the trenches so deep that the seeds must have thought they were never going to see the light of day.

Looking back, that period of time had many pleasurable memories. The children were getting older and easier to look after. Hard work was showing its rewards in the garden, and the house was aired with almost all the rooms opened up again and each of the children now having a room of their own.

Derek and I married in spring 1981. We had a small family wedding, with just relations invited to a reception at the farm. We were both by now very sure of our commitment and the children were happy for us. There was to be no fuss but, as is typical, my mother was able to make it extra special for us by buying a lovely wedding cake and beautiful flowers. Both my parents have always supported me; I had a very happy childhood with a close relationship with both my parents, which has lasted through these later years. I hoped that my new family would be as lucky.

With so much freedom in those days, the school holidays passed quickly for the children, what with the paddling pool and swings to play on; with so much space, we very often had about eight to ten children with us as the local village children came up to play. Haymaking time meant that packed lunches could be taken out to the fields, and cold salad suppers eaten at the end of balmy days when the hay had been hauled home.

Fishing was something that all the children enjoyed, even Kelly, and as one of our fields was bordered by the River Brue, many a summer's day was spent on the riverbank. When they returned home one afternoon, Barry was annoyed as Simon, who was still only seven, had spent all day casting and reeling in, constantly getting in a tangle which Barry had to sort out: 'And he's not coming again unless he learns some patience' was the passing shot as he stomped to his bedroom. The following day, carrying out a basket of washing, I came across Simon sitting like a gnome on the bit of old fence by our duck pond, a stagnant pond devoid of plants or fish. With his rod dangling over the water, he was sitting silently, almost motionless. 'You won't catch anything in there', I called. 'I know', he replied. Walking towards him, I said: 'What are you doing then?' Back came the serious answer – 'I'm learning patience.'

Our reputation with poultry was beginning to spread and we found that we were now giving advice, and that people were visiting to buy stock or fertile eggs. I even had one frantic lady ring at 11.30 one evening – her broody hen was hatching out and what should she do?? I gathered from the conversation that almost every hour she had been lifting the poor hen up to see what was happening and at last one of the eggs was cracking. My advice (given quite politely) was to leave the hen alone, go to bed and check the results the next morning. Peace and quiet was all the hen needed to do the job properly.

Hens and ducks will usually lay at the age of six months, but birds in general tie in with nature and the seasons: this means that if a duck is hatched in April or May she will not be six months old until October, and because at this time the days are getting short, if she is kept free-range she will probably delay starting to produce eggs until the following spring when the days start to lengthen.

A man came and purchased six Khaki Campbell ducklings and we told him they should lay at around six months of age. This was unfortunately to be one occasion when the ducks decided to wait until the following spring. Rather irate, he returned when they were seven months old, quite concerned that nothing had been produced. We explained the situation, which he grudgingly accepted; but meanwhile as we had walked around he had seen some hens he liked which could go with the few odd ones he had at home. Offering them to him cheaper due to the non-arrival of any eggs, he left a happier man. One month later he returned. Not only was just one duck laying, but the rotten chickens that we had sold him had taught his odd few how to fly over the fence. He had

had to erect higher fences to protect his vegetable garden, which had been ravaged. He now wanted a drake so that when these blessed ducks *did* decide to lay he could hatch some fertile eggs. We had several in one brood and were happy to supply him with one, once again at a reduced price with sincere apologies for our hens' bad manners.

One week later he returned. Looking uncomfortable, he stood in the doorway with the drake tucked under his arm. Could I possibly help him as he thought the bird was ill? Placing the bird on the table to inspect it, I noticed that the penis, usually carried internally, was lying swollen by the anus. It had obviously become infected. 'Do you know what's wrong with it?' he stuttered. 'Well,' I answered, 'It's a male, isn't it? And THAT should not be on the outside.' I explained that, due to the infection, it was not possible to massage it back in, and unfortunately the bird would need to be seen by a vet. I recommended our own vet (yet another distant relation), and he departed to get the bird attended to. A phone call two days later had me speaking to him again. Absolutely mortified, he explained that the vet had cleaned it up and stitched it back in, but had told him that if the drake did not pass anything within 24 hours to bring it back for the stitch to be taken out. Unfortunately the poor bird died and he was quite convinced he should have taken it back earlier to have the stitch removed. Trying to pacify him, I told him I was sure it was probably shock that had killed him, and that although it had been most unfortunate we had several spare drakes and he was more than welcome to another one. He did, in fact, come and collect one, which was a brother to the one that died; and that was the last we saw of him.

A month later, our vet was called out to see to a difficult calving, and as is usually the case, when everything is sorted out, we all returned to the farmhouse kitchen for a coffee. I was filling the kettle and Derek was sorting the cups out as the vet was washing his hands. 'Hey!', he said, 'You know the man you sent to me with the drake, you know the one suffering from the common term Dick-Out?' (Such a way with words!) Derek and I looked at each other and smiled – we certainly did. 'He came back the next week with one with exactly the same condition!' I smiled and explained that we had in fact given him another drake, which was a brother to the first one. 'Probably a genetic fault', the vet said. 'Do you know, when he was in the surgery with the second one, he glanced furtively about him to make sure no one could hear, and asked, "Do you think . . .", he said, "Do you think I've got a tight duck??"'

The winter of 1981 and spring of 1982 was about to throw everything it possibly could at us. November was very wet, followed by storms and high winds in December when exceptionally high tides took their toll. The sea wall was breached and many, many areas were badly flooded, some as high as between four and six feet, and it took several days to abate. Several houses near here are built on clay with no proper foundation as they were so old; these were so badly damaged that they were never lived in again. We were very lucky that it did not affect us – within a mile of us there were boats moored up to the bus stops for people to get back to where they lived. We were without electricity for three days, but as we had the Rayburn and gas heaters we were all right. (I was worried about the tropical fish – but we covered the tank with a blanket and they survived!) It was rather nice to go back to candles and playing board games in the evening as there was no television. Soon most things were back to normal, but there were several long-term problems from the flooding that took quite a time to be rectified. Many families were unable to return to their houses until the following year, and quite a few lost all their possessions with Christmas having to be spent in temporary homes. There was a lot of salt damage to the fields that had been flooded by the sea, and crop growth was inhibited for the next few years.

Most of the farms on the Somerset Levels are dairy farms as the land is too wet to grow any other crop except grass. Dairy cows are brought in for the winter, usually by late October, and the farmer would expect to turn his cows out in the spring, which would be mid-April. Everything is geared to this. During the summer enough hay and silage is stored to feed the cows while the grass is not growing in the cold winter, in order to maintain the milk yield. Hence by April the stocks of hay and silage are low because usually it is just a few weeks before the cows are back in the fields. This was not to be so in the spring of 1982. The rains began to fall in March, continued through April and even into May. Farmers ran completely out of stored feed and the limited supply of hay and silage that was available was fetching incredible prices. As farmers were forced to turn the cows out into the fields, at least during the day, to find grass to eat, the land was being churned up into mud. Down on the moors, things were even worse where farmers were unable to reach cattle by tractors. Everything was against them. Without the supply of good quality feeds, milk yields dropped; this meant that the monthly milk cheque, which is what most farmers live off, was smaller than usual. This was the kind of year that farmers would have to write off as a bad year, but there was to be an even more catastrophic effect from this problem two years later. Even when the land started to dry, where the fields had been churned to mud the grass took a long time to recover; many farmers were very short of grass and even had to sell animals. We managed, but only by renting extra grass – additional costs we had not allowed for. We were carrying a lot of stock as we were nearly at the point of our own heifers calving in to join the milking herd, which would then increase our milk yield and we could see our way to paying off the large overdraft that had been increasing at the bank.

What was to happen in 1984 was one of the greatest turning points in farming history. The government, headed by Margaret Thatcher, took steps to deal with the European milk surplus, and with hardly any notice whatsoever, milk quotas were introduced and implemented immediately. We had even had a Ministry adviser out to see us three weeks earlier, and he was completely unaware of milk quotas being brought in. To be quite honest, there was sheer panic throughout the dairy industry with little media coverage. All farmers were notified that their milk production was to be based on 10 per cent less than they produced from March 1982 to February 1983. This, as we have said before, was already classed as a bad year, so you were looking at almost a 20 per cent reduction in milk production. It made no difference if you had been on a government grading-up scheme – they had changed their policies and it was just hard luck. For every litre of milk produced and sent to the dairy over and above your quota you were fined more than the milk was worth, so in fact it was cheaper just to pour it away. Prices of cows were devalued from averaging £600 per head to £400 if you were lucky, as nobody wanted to buy dairy cows. Calf prices dropped from £100–125 down to £25–50, again if you could find a buyer. Basically, our stock was devalued by £20,000 overnight. Farming magazines showed in-calf cows being sent to slaughter, a thing never done before, by farmers worried that they would produce too much milk and no one was interested in buying the animals alive. Yet this never hit the national newspapers. Suddenly the farmers were in the wrong for over-producing, many went bankrupt, others sold up; some even committed suicide, unable

17

to see a way forward in a lifestyle that had been in their family for generations before them, but that was no longer viable.

'No problem,' said someone, sitting on a chair in government, 'after all, they only work 18 hours a day – let them diversify!'

We seriously had to think of another form of income. Desperately hoping to keep the farm going, we looked at several options. One was that I could have gone and found a job, but with the four children still taking a lot of my time and the different crises that arose at times on the farm, it seemed impractical. Perhaps we could do some caravans – tidy the place up and even let people visit the farm. People had said how much they enjoyed visiting when they came to look at the poultry. Derek did not think that this idea would appeal to people; but when a stiff letter arrived from the bank, the decision was made for us. We were entering the world of tourism, for better or worse – here we come!

2

The Animals Came in Two by Two

The farm lent itself to being a tourist attraction. Over 300 years old, it is now a listed building and creates a lovely atmosphere of history. The house was probably originally built by a rich yeoman. It would have had a front door with one room on the right containing a range for the kitchen, and another room on the left for the sitting room. On the first floor were two bedrooms built above the main rooms, and on the second floor were two servants' rooms; the original staircase and banister are still in existence on this floor. The curved balusters are now painted in gloss white (much to the horror of the man who came and dated the house!). Had the originals still existed in the lower part of the house, there would have been carvings of fruit decorating them. We had opened up these servants' rooms as we had slowly renovated the house; in them we discovered the small brass bells with their wire pulls which had probably been blessed many times in years gone by!

The beams in this part of the house were incredibly difficult to sand down as, although thickly coated in lime, they are solid elm underneath. The family must have outgrown the house very quickly as extensions were added to either end of it. On the far end a salting cellar was added, with two bedrooms above. All the meat would have been salted here to preserve it, as these were the days well before refrigerators were invented!

At the other end of the house, an extension was built as a dairy to house the large cheese vat; this was a room where the milk was taken in to be made into cheese. In this dairy you can still see where the floor has been worn away from the constant rolling of churns to bring the milk in. Up above was the cheese room, where the cheese racks were still to be found; these used to store all the cheeses which were pulled through a trap in the ceiling by hoist, up into the room, and then placed on the racks. They would be turned once a day, and it would be six months before the cheese would be fit for market. Both Cheddar and Caerphilly cheese were made at the farm.

By the time the Kidners arrived at the farm, the farmhouse had another extension on the back; this one was obviously built in a later period as the beams in this part of the house are pitched pine and the ceilings are much lower. This meant that the house now consisted of kitchen, three main rooms, dairy and cheese room, cellar, bathroom and eight bedrooms. There is a second staircase, made of cheaper wood, which would have been used by the servants. The risers are worn away in the centre, through constant use.

Derek's father, Jack, came to the farm in the 1930s as a lad of fifteen, when Grandad Kidner became the tenant of the farm and brought his family to East Huntspill. Sadly, Derek's father died in 1991. He would tell many stories of their time on the farm. He could remember going to the market with his father, taking the cheeses by horse and cart into Highbridge, which at that time was a thriving town, with both a port and a railway station; at that time, Highbridge had the largest cheese market in Europe. There was also a large bacon factory, as all the farms that made cheese would keep pigs to fatten on the whey that is a by-product of cheese-making.

All this, of course, is well before the days of the Milk Marketing Board. Milk deliveries, in those days, consisted of a man going round with a churn on a cart; the milk was ladled out into the jugs belonging to the customers waiting for their supply.

In our backhouse can be seen the fresh water pump, sadly no longer working – one day, we must try and find the well. A small chimney services the old copper where the washing used to be done, with a small grate underneath for a fire to heat the water. Not far away, I am pleased to say, stands my automatic. A stark contrast, with the old copper and mangle on one side and the automatic plus dryer on the other side of the room!

A square of outbuildings surrounds the yard in front of the house, which in the nineteenth century would have housed all the cattle in the winter. Later, in the following century, cowsheds were built further away from the farm to be used for winter quarters so that the animals were not kept literally on your doorstep.

It was my idea to plant a tree in the middle of the yard, with a seat round it, to make the yard look more attractive. Derek usually takes a couple of years before he gets used to things being different; he had already backed the car into the seat twice before he eventually managed to write it off completely, damaging the car quite badly, on the third occasion. He had just been told that our bull had escaped – being fully aware of the dangers of a bull on the loose, Derek swung into action. Key in ignition, straight into reverse and backed right into the seat with such a force that it collapsed, leaving the tree slightly bending to the left. (My fault, of course, for planting it there!) The insurance form sent in for the damages to the car read: 'I was in a hurry because my bull had escaped and I reversed into a seat that did not used to be there!'

Cobblestoned stables still stand next to the large cider house, a reminder of the days when heavy horses carried out the work before tractors became the order of the day. In Grandad Kidner's day, they had a large horse called Ginger, who could, by all accounts, be quite evil, and they basically used to draw lots as to who had to ride him up to the blacksmith. The journey up was easy, but once his shoes were done and he was on the home stretch, he was away. It would take at least two to hold him down, to give time for the poor soul who was riding him home to get on. Grasping the reins tightly, and gripping with the legs, the rider would give the 'all clear', and once released, old Ginger would go like the clappers all the way home. ''Twer no good if som'at were i'nt way', he wouldn't stop, they just had to get out of the way. It took at least three glasses of cider to get over the experience!

We cleared out all of the sheds in the next few years, discovering many things that had lain forgotten for many decades, some even before the time of Grandad Kidner. Old machinery, the hand wheels from the cider press, a very long pump that would be thrown into the rhines to pump up water in the days when steam engines were used in the fields. We even found a needle in a haystack: a long 12-foot needle with a tiny hook on the end which was used for testing the temperature in the centre of a haystack to guard against it catching fire. We found so much to put on display and for visitors to compare with the modern methods now used.

To start with we only had part of the farm open, mainly the yard area. Pigs were the first new acquisition. Part of the stables has been altered to house the pigs, with a window so that visitors could watch the sows farrowing. Derek bought two saddleback pigs due to farrow any minute. Never having had anything to do with pigs before, I was surprised at just how big they were: at least five foot long and reaching up to my waist. People are always free with advice and stories, and one local told us how vicious they can be, and how he had heard of someone who had gone in with a group of sows and never came out again! (It does your confidence a power of good, little gems like these.)

They were lovely quiet pigs, pink and black with ears that flopped over their faces. I can remember seeing a small schoolchild, with a clipboard, trying to answer her questionnaire which asked her what the pig's eyes looked like. The sow was standing by the gate: squatting down beside the pig, the girl lifted the sow's ear and carefully drew the eye as the pig stood patiently waiting for her to finish.

When the first sow farrowed, she had eighteen piglets. To start with piglets will suckle from any teat, but after the first couple of days each piglet has its own teat. Those that feed from the front get the most milk, and the weaker piglets have the teats at the back. Inevitably, there was a runt who began to look very poorly and I did not have the heart to see it go hungry, so it was brought in by the Rayburn for warmth and to be bottle-fed. Sadie was to be my first little pig that I hand-reared. Pigs can become very tame and will almost behave like dogs. Sadie was quite happy living in the kitchen and we even trained her to go outside to go to the toilet. She was joined by the runt from the second litter when the other saddleback farrowed, a little boy that we called Splodge. They would both play in between naps and then crash out on the carpet for another sleep. It seemed perfectly normal to have them in the house while they were young, in the same way as we look after anything poorly in the warm, until it is well enough to go back outside. I suppose the sight of two piglets asleep on the carpet in the kitchen must have seemed amusing, and once the newspapers heard about it, we were inundated with photographers wanting to take pictures. The story became a little embroidered: one national newspaper even reported that Sadie had her own chair by the fire and watched television with us!

We did have television cameras out to do a short piece for the local news programme, and for the sake of publicity, I am ashamed to say, the family were filmed eating bowls of cereal at the table complete with Splodge eating out of a bowl too. (Needless to say, Derek was not around at the time, otherwise I am sure he would have joined in!) The piglets, however, had the last laugh, as by now they were entering into the spirit of things and ready for fun. Grabbing the wire attached to the sound fluffball, they charged outside to play, complete with camera crew in tow, desperate to get their equipment back in one piece. That piece unfortunately was not shown on the news item!

We started a herd of goats, trying to have a variety of breeds for people to see. The golden Guernseys are a lovely honey colour and the small pygmy goats are real characters. These were soon joined by saanen goats and eventually angora goats as well. Goats and rabbits are the two things that we get offered more than any other animals. The idea of having a goat to keep the grass down is not a good one at all as a goat will eat just about everything, flowers, hedgerow, even bramble, before it will finally resort to eating grass. They are also the one animal that is never content to stay one side of a fence, and they will go to extraordinary lengths to scale any barrier just to find out what is on the other side; if it proves to be uninteresting, the goat will then stand and bleat that it wants to go back, but never seems to have the intelligence to remember how it got out in the first place. Stupid they may be, but always friendly, and they are a firm favourite with the visitors. My only criticism is that instead of waiting for the handful of feed, given the chance they will swipe the whole bag!

One lad who worked for us on a Work Opportunity Scheme was Tim. He was very interested in ferrets and offered to give us some as an exhibit. Having heard all the stories about them, I was slightly hesitant but eventually Tim won me round. Derek thought it was quite a good idea, but did not want to have anything to do with them. Tim seemed to think they would be all right in the old cheese vat which had steep metal sides that they would be unable to climb out of. Covering the floor of the vat with shavings, and putting tubes in for them to play with, the pen was made ready and we waited for their arrival.

When Tim brought them out to us, I was very taken with them.

Ferrets are related to the badger, and have a very similar musky smell due to the presence of musk glands. They have a very small face with a pointed nose and tiny ears. Their bodies are very long, similar to a stoat's but much bigger with short legs that have very fine claws, which they can use to climb with great agility. We were given a white female with a youngster of the same colour and another female with the dark brown colourings of a polecat. Very inquisitive, they seemed like quicksilver as they looped round your arms, wriggling all the time. When they were placed into their new pen they danced with excitement, prancing and pushing their heads along in the shavings. The tubes were explored, with heads popping out and then darting back in, before taking the plunge and charging right out to disappear down another tube. They certainly were fascinating to watch. Giving me their diet sheet, Tim went through a few details on how to look after them which included how to get them to release if they decide to bite (!). When a ferret does bite properly, it will lock its jaws and the only way you can get it to release the victim is to squeeze hard at the hinge of the jaw – hopefully it will relax its grip. With this vital information I was left to manage on my own.

Over the next few days I got to know them but still did not really have complete confidence in handling them. However, they were a great attraction in the dairy. At this time we had got the cheese racks down from upstairs and had all the old cheese-making equipment on show. The ferrets were in the cheese vat along by the window; and underneath the open-tread wooden staircase there were wooden boxes, where I had broody chickens sitting on fertile eggs. The broodies would sit tight on the eggs, incubating them, and there was no need to worry about children touching them, because any attempt to do so would be defended by a peck.

Derek was busy doing the morning milking a few days later, and all the children were sitting having breakfast before they left for school. Suddenly a dreadful noise came from the dairy. Flying in to find out what had happened, I came face to face with the cream ferret who had managed to scale the side of the cheese vat and had attacked one of the broody chickens. Despite the fact that the chicken was almost four times the size of the ferret, it was already dead with the ferret's jaws anchored around the base of its head. Feathers rolled on the floor from the attack and five other very frightened hens poked their heads out of their boxes. I grabbed the ferret before it escaped, its jaws remaining clamped to

Pauline and Derek, with ragamuffin Barney, everybody's friend

Pauline and two of the original badger cubs, Willow and Primrose

Pet donkey Mathilda, with daughter Mildred

Local expert Sidney Lane gives a demonstration of bee keeping to some young
visitors to the farm

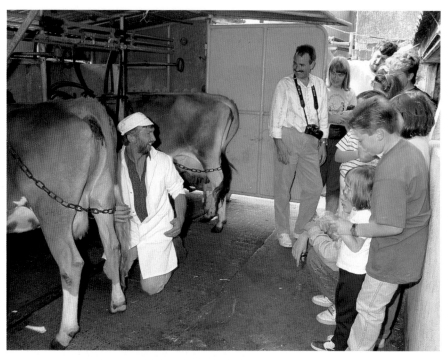

Derek demonstrates how to milk a cow

Simon giving a talk about owls with the help of Sage

Jo, a female tawny owl

Batman and Robin! Baby robin enjoying lunch (top) and a young pipistrelle (below)

Timmy, the tawny owlet orphan, in the sick room, where he enjoyed looking out at the visitors *Below* Young barn owls – even at one day old they are ready to eat meat

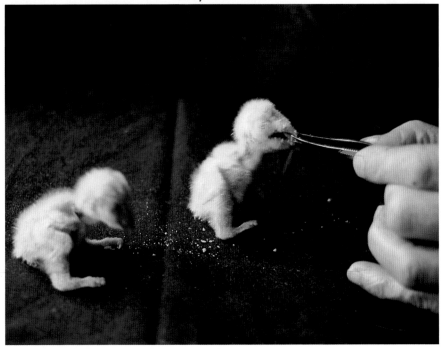

Four young barn owls look surprised at the camera

the hen, but even with the full weight of the bird dangling from its mouth, the ferret refused to let go. Squeezing at the base of the jaw, as Tim had shown me, I eventually managed to get the hen free, but it was beyond help. Extremely nervously, I placed the ferret in an old bird cage that was in the room above, grateful that it had not retaliated by having a go at me for taking its prize. Carrying the cage indoors, I placed it in the room opposite the kitchen and closed the door.

First things first: the children had to get to school, then I would sort out how to contain the ferrets properly. By the time the children had finished their breakfast after all the upheaval, and departed on their bikes, Derek was in for his cooked breakfast. As we sat eating, I told Derek what had happened and how, at the moment, the ferret that had escaped was in the front room in a cage. The scratching at the door that followed made it quite clear that the ferret was no longer in its cage. Carefully, I opened the door and went in, thinking Derek would follow to help. By this time the ferret had moved away from the door and was standing on the back of the armchair. It was obvious, by the fact that it was now black, that it had already been up the chimney. On seeing me, the ferret launched itself from the chair and landed full square on my front. My immediate response was to lift it off and place it on the ground; straight away it clawed its way right up my trouser leg and back onto my jumper. Not happy with this situation at all, I again lifted it off and put it on the ground, to which it repeated the run up my body. Advice was at hand. Standing with his head poking around the door, which was protecting the remainder of his body, Derek said: 'I think it's just frightened, and it's coming to you for company.' That could well be, was my reply, but I was not at all happy with the situation; and placing the ferret once more on the ground, I pushed Derek back into the kitchen, whipped round to join him, and shut the door quickly!

Needless to say, I have become far more adept at handling ferrets now and enjoy taking them to shows where they cause a lot of interest. They really do not deserve the bad press that they are given. Maybe I am tempting fate, but I have never been bitten by any of our ferrets, and we now have fifteen. We do not breed them nor do we buy them – they are all ones found wandering, escaped or thrown out and taken into the RSPCA, or they come from call-outs that we have responded to. Now we have a large pen for them, with tunnels and branches, plus an outside area too

— a pen they can't escape from! I very often take them to shows and people will come and fuss them. Everyone has heard of ferrets but very few know what they really look like. One lady came up to me and fussed a ferret I was holding. 'Isn't he lovely?' she said. 'Yes', was my reply. She gave it a stroke.

'What's his name?' she asked. The one I had at that time was Basil.

Tickling its ears, her next question was, 'What is it?'

'It's a ferret,' I answered, to which she screamed and was gone, and I did not see her again.

The only problem with taking them to shows is that they do have this musky smell; and when I take my break at lunchtime, with other exhibitors, I make sure that I sit next to someone who knows what I have been doing, otherwise they might disapprove of my perfume!

Ferrets have been used by man for catching rabbits for over 2,000 years. Even now they are still worked in the countryside.

. . . the ferret launched itself from the chair . . .

26

Nets are placed over the bolt-holes of a rabbit burrow and the ferret is placed down the tunnels to chase the rabbits out. We do not work ours, though; they are just for show and live quite harmoniously as a group.

The polecat, a British mammal, is related to the ferret and was at one time widespread across the British Isles, but due to persecution, mainly by gamekeepers, they were almost eradicated, only maintaining a foothold in Wales. Their fur – called fitch fur – was often used on collars of coats. Happily, they do seem to be increasing in numbers and are beginning to be found in more areas.

The caravan and camping side of the farm was slow to take off, but we always had a few caravans in. The tents were invariably those of foreign visitors touring the country and we met some very interesting people. We had a lovely Dutch family here for quite a few months, and they have become firm family friends whom we see usually each year. Mas is a tall striking blonde woman with a lovely wide smile. Marien, again tall, but dark-haired, has a severe face which softens when he smiles; the first time we saw him, he was dressed in a long trench coat which gave an impression of a Russian spy! Despite the language barrier, the two children, Dagmar and Yort, immediately got on very well with our two boys Daniel and Simon, sign language causing a lot of laughter.

Mas and Marien had come to the country to learn about the exercises used to stimulate brain-injured children at a nearby Institute. During the time they were staying with us, we were haymaking and Marien was keen to help. We were hoping to bring some loads in from the fields in the afternoon and Marien was talking to us, explaining that they were going to see Stonehenge. 'We leave at 12 noon', he said, 'er, but we come back to 'elp you wiz da hay, ja?'

Derek said that would be fine, thinking to himself that they would not be back in time, as it would take at least two hours to get there and two hours back, and we were hoping to start around 3 p.m.

We waved goodbye to the family just before midday and finished the day's chores. Just after 3.30 p.m. Derek towed the first load of hay back from the fields and was surprised to see that the Dutch family were already back.

'You didn't take long,' Derek remarked to Marien as he strode towards him.

'I drive fast,' said Marien, shrugging his shoulders; 'We go, we see, we come back.'

Surprised, Derek asked, 'Didn't you stop at all?'

'Oh, ja,' nodded Marien, 'We stop twice – once to look at dead badger and once to let Yort be sick. You ready now?'

Some sightseer! They return briefly each year to update on further developments of exercises at the Institute for Brain Injured Children and we usually have the pleasure of seeing them and catching up with their family news. One day we shall get to Holland to visit them ourselves.

During their stay here, they would walk out into the fields each evening and had the pleasure of watching a sow badger with her cubs most evenings at a large sett a few fields away from us. The Dutch are very fond of badgers.

I once went to a Badger Conference, a weekend event, at which a talk was given by two young ladies from a badger group which had been involved with the construction of a new major road. Having surveyed the area for badgers, they had pinpointed areas where badger territorial paths crossed the route of the new road which therefore necessitated the building of badger tunnels under the road, to avoid badger deaths and the possibility of road accidents. The job entailed a considerable amount of time and effort on their part, to oversee the project and to make sure that the badger tunnels were not forgotten as this was not considered an important issue in the construction. They also had to fight hard to be given any decent length of fencing to guide the badgers into the tunnels, as it was 'all extra cost'. However, thanks to their determination, the tunnels were included in the building of the new road, and hopefully the badgers have managed to adapt to having a busy road near their setts and, with the safety of tunnels, have not been killed by continuing to use their same paths. We were impressed with what the badger group had achieved, and realized how necessary it is to monitor the construction work all the way through to make sure that the tunnels are put in the right places and built in the right way.

The following day, the Dutch sector of the badger group gave a talk explaining what they had done in Holland. They showed how they raise orphan cubs, their surveying work and also their involvement with road construction. We were shown slides of an area where a new road through the countryside was being built. Several tunnels were built as underpasses for the badgers, with metre upon metre of fencing to guide the badgers towards the underpasses away from the danger of the roads. 'Of course,' said the Dutch representative, 'We do not 'ave badgers in dis area, but 'ope if dey do come, dat dey will use ze tunnels.' A slight difference in attitude!

In the same year, we had about five caravans in the field and a New Zealand couple arrived with backpacks, and asked if they could camp overnight. Having shown them the field, I carried on with the afternoon feeding. Meeting up later with the young man from New Zealand, we were talking and he mentioned that he would rather sleep in the open than in a tent, and I suggested that he slept on the couch in the table tennis room which we had for campers at that time. He took me up on the offer and settled in the games room. Later, as I was shutting up the poultry at the end of the day, I saw that the young girl from New Zealand had still pitched her tent in the field by the caravans on her own. I could see why the young man felt claustrophobic in the tent, as it consisted of just a sleeping bag in a coffin shape with a canvas hood that was raised only about 18 inches from the ground, just around the head and shoulders area.

The next morning, I was standing passing the time of day with one of the visitors staying in the caravans, and the young girl from New Zealand passed us, bidding good morning, and going into the toilets. Nudging me, the visitor from the caravans said: 'You see that young woman – it's been the talk of the site – have you seen their tent?' Nodding, I smiled. 'There's only one way', he said, 'that they could have both fitted in that!' I did not spoil their amusement by explaining that the young man had slept in the games room.

The farm was becoming ever busier with visitors each season. Unfortunately, the more visitors, the more facilities were needed and, as yet, the tourist side of the farm was not paying. We had come to a time when we had to make decisions. The bank would no longer back us with both ventures. We knew that the dairy herd would never resolve our problems and there was potential in the tourist side so, with much heartache, the decision had to be made to sell our milking herd. It was a very sad morning when Derek and I brought the cows in for the last time, ready for the sale to be held at the farm. Cows that we had reared, ones that Derek had cared for over many years, were finally to go. Neither of us spoke very much and it was one of the few times that we argued. It was almost as if we needed to hurt each other because we hurt so much inside. People who make sweeping statements about farmers who keep animals purely as breeding machines don't even begin to understand the affinity that grows over years of caring and husbandry.

We closed the gate after the last one went through, and they all stood in the collecting yard. Hurdles had been placed out ready to become the sale ring. The cows bellowed, sensing that something was different. Putting his arms around me, Derek squeezed me tight. There was no need for words, we both shared the same feelings; I don't think words could even have expressed the loss of all those years of work building up the herd. Turning our backs on the scene, almost to try and shut it out, we walked slowly back to the house to wait for everyone to turn up. It is one day I don't like to remember.

The money that we raised from selling the cows helped pay off the overdraft and we had some capital left to plough back into making a business of the Open Farm. We needed a tearoom, and after much thought decided that as our two eldest children had now left home, we would move upstairs and turn the ground floor of the farmhouse into a tearoom. Still wanting it to appear very much like our home, we left much of our antique furniture downstairs. There is a large inglenook fireplace in one of the front rooms and the floors have been taken back to the old flagstones. In the kitchen there is a lovely 8-foot-long pine dresser which, when I first came to the farm, was painted green and yellow and discarded in the backhouse, used for keeping tools in. We had it stripped back to the original pine and it now has pride of place in the kitchen with brass saucepans and decorative plates on the shelves. A pine counter built into the kitchen is used as the service area for the tearoom – a far cry from the kitchen I first came to many years ago with its plastic curtains and bare light bulb! Extra toilets had to be built, and finally the cider house was changed into a Visitor Centre, partially funded by the Countryside Commission and Somerset County Council.

The schoolchildren, when they visited, often asked if we had any horses, so we decided to have some Shetland ponies. Dinky was the first to arrive. She was a tubby dark brown pony with a white blaze down her nose and, as she had been running with a stallion, we were hoping she may have a foal, but were not too bothered one way or another.

With the numbers of animals ever increasing, we were beginning to need more help. A couple called Andy and Lisa would come and muck in any time we needed help. Andy and Lisa lived locally and, we had come to know them through a shared interest in poultry; they themselves keep all sorts of animals. It was through them that we obtained our chipmunks, which chase around in an aviary near the kitchen window. Lisa was helping us when Mike Hayes, another local vet, came to inject some piglets. Mike has a very keen sense of humour and, as well as being a qualified vet, is extremely clever at carpentry. (Although not very good at finishing things – we are still waiting for the honey spoons he promised to make!) He is fun to work with and nearly always has time for that cup of coffee when he has finished!

Pigs are not very easy to handle and the sows become very upset when separated from their young, which you have to do for the purpose of injecting. The piglets make a terrible squealing noise when they are picked up, and if the sow was around, she would attack you. We had shut the two sows out into the outside area of the pen and had all the piglets shut inside with us. There was Derek, myself, Lisa, and Mike the vet. Injecting each piglet in turn, we were marking them with colour spray so that we could tell which ones had been done. The noise was horrendous, piglets squealing and both the sows roaring their objections to the proceedings outside.

Mike needed a fresh needle and decided to sprint across the outside yard to the metal gate once the sows had their backs turned. They may have had their backs turned but they were certainly watching, and the first glimpse of Mike in his brown coat and green wellies creeping across the pen was enough to incite lightening responses from both sows. They charged dramatically with jaws open, ready to take a chunk out of his legs. A man in true desperation, Mike high-jumped the gate with such speed that any budding gymnast would have applauded. It was just that the toe of his wellie did not quite clear the gate that made this spectacular leap into a hilarious situation. With one foot caught going over, Mike rolled head over heels to fall squarely in the sludgy puddle of water that had collected in front of the gate; and, of course, as he hit the puddle with such force, the water shot into the air only to fall back onto the deflated muddy heap that once was a respectable vet.

Even the sows had got out of the way of the disgusting spray and were standing in the corner of the pen, tails swishing. Hauling himself up by the rungs of the gate, Mike remarked on the closeness of his encounter in the most colourful of languages. He stood with his curly hair dripping, but in true British form, he pushed up his sleeves and wiped as much muck off his coat with his hands as he could, and marched to his car to get the fresh needles. A round of applause broke out from the pig house together with unsympathetic laughter. There were only a few more to do, so sluicing off his hands under the tap, he braved the pen again; but by this time the sows were no longer interested as the piglets had gone quiet. The work was finished with the banter of how impressed we were with his athletics and with remarks about the pungent smell that was now in the air. Lisa in particular gave him a hard time. Job over, the sows were put back with their piglets and we all made our way back to the house for a coffee. Mike was doing his best to clean up. The conversation went on to Dinky and how we were hoping she was in foal. Mike explained that the best way to find out was to have a urine test done – catch some urine as she passes some in the stable and send it in to the surgery. We explained that Dinky never seemed to urinate in her stable.

'That's easy,' Mike said, 'All you have to do is take a jug, tickle her t'ainter and she will pee in a matter of minutes.'

We all looked at him curiously. And just WHERE was her 't'ainter', we wanted to know?

'Under her tail, it t'aint her arse and it t'aint her fanny, it's the bit in the middle,' he explained, in a very matter-of-fact way. We all looked for the hint of a smile but he was deadly serious.

'Honestly,' he said to Lisa, 'get a jug and I guarantee, she'll pass a specimen almost straight away.' He then carried on talking to Derek about the diet for the pigs. Lisa fetched a jug and off she went. As the conversation lulled, I expressed my surprise that tickling a pony's – er, 't'ainter' would make her pass urine.

'No, it doesn't,' replied Mike, 'but it will teach Lisa a lesson for laughing at me!' He grinned.

Lisa came back with an empty jug and a red face! Dinky never did foal, but we eventually got a friend for her, a small male Shetland called Tom Thumb. Tom is a golden colour with a very long mane, but he has always been nervous. We also have an old pony who retired to us at the age of 25. He is called Darkie, though he sports quite a few grey hairs now!

It was while Andy and Lisa still came to the farm that we

acquired Barney. Sadly Chutney, the Jack Russell, was run over and died; it was a few months later that Lisa and Andy came out to us with a young dog who was about six months of age. They were looking after him as he had been cruelly treated, but he was so soppy. Barney is thought to be a cross between a bearded collie and a labrador as he is a very thick-coated dog. He is the type of mongrel that everybody loves, a true farm dog. Simon took him on as his dog, although Barney tries to share himself between Simon and Derek. He is with Simon when Si is home from school, or else Barney follows Derek around.

Following the van or tractor, he is into everything. He even helped when it came to sheep-shearing time, and TRIED to help with rounding up the sheep; unfortunately, he has no sense of timing or direction and Derek finally shut him in the van, to keep him out of the way. From there he sat in the driver's seat and barked to encourage the rest of us in our endeavours to herd the sheep into the pen. By the time the shearing started, he was worn out with all the excitement and sat panting, while Clive, our cousin, sheared the sheep. Simon was there helping roll up the fleeces. Clive and Simon, between the two of them, decided to shear Barney as he was so hot, but they only did his body. Laughing at him, they came up for tea; there was this stupid-looking animal with a head and ruff like a lion, a smooth body and then fluffy legs and tail. Joining in with the fun, Barney pranced around sporting his new haircut. He was dispatched to the kennels the next day to be clipped properly. He is now done regularly, so he varies between being a scruffbag and a smooth-haired dog. His girth has widened considerably, now that he is able to recognize a picnic hamper and has learnt the art of begging.

Somerset County Council and the Countryside Commission became involved with the farm and helped finance the creation of a Visitor Centre in the old cider house. The ground floor area is given to explaining the history of our family, the location of the farm and also the typical farming methods of this area. We tried very hard not to make the content too concentrated, and it has been made more fun by large cartoons drawn on the interpretation boards and a scale model of the farm with areas that light up to explain the usage of different buildings. The top floor is used to explain the Levels and moors of Somerset. A large 8-foot model depicts the area and a short film with lighting effects demonstrates the history of the area and shows the flooding that encourages a rich variety of wildlife in our part of the country. By now, the whole of the farm was open to the public and the homeground, divided into paddocks, shows the different breeds of animals that we keep.

We were offered some white-faced woodland sheep and, as they were quite rare, Derek decided to buy four. Setting off in our ramshackle van, he hoped to make it there before it was dark. It was winter and the evenings were drawing in quite quickly. He had been late leaving as we had a problem with one of the cows. Luckily, he found the smallholding quite easily and loaded the sheep without too much fuss. They were quite a large breed, and four of them in the back of our red van was quite a squeeze. Still, at least if they were in quite tight, they would not roll around in the back of the van as it moved. It was now just after 5 p.m. and Derek was getting caught up with the rush-hour traffic of people on their way home after work. Nearing Bridgwater, he decided to cut through one of the back lanes and miss the town centre. The sheep so far had travelled quietly and, lulled into a false sense of security, he had almost forgotten they were in the back. The sheep had horns, and one had manoeuvred itself near to the door and got its horn wrapped round the cord to the back door latch. Derek was surprised by the sudden rush of cold air and was somewhat mystified by two sounds of things bumping, until he realized to his horror that the back door had swung open and two sheep had made a very fast exit.

Pulling in quickly, Derek stopped the van, quietly praying that nobody had been too close behind. He found he was in a quiet road, with no street lighting and – so far – little traffic. There had been a man in a car behind but he had managed to miss the two flying woolley objects and had pulled up also, to see if he could assist in any way. Quickly shutting the back doors of the van to confine the two remaining sheep, Derek's round-up began. It was very kind of the man to have stopped, but herding animals does not come naturally and this man was lacking in any natural ability whatsoever other than to comment repeatedly 'oh, dear' as Derek, trying to corner the sheep with him, kept seeing the ewes shoot past him. Eventually one sheep ran into the hedge: oblivious of the bramble. Derek followed suit and grabbed two handfuls of fleece – he had caught one escapee at least. He dragged the resentful sheep back to the van, but the nightmare was only just starting. Squeezing the ewe against the van, Derek tried to make one hand available to open the van door, but immediately realized he had no more hands left to hold back the sheep that were already in the van. Throwing the van door open, he lunged forward to push the other two sheep back inside, lifting the escapee bodily in to block their efforts of release. Slamming the door shut, he leaned back against it to regain his breath after his exertion, only to watch the remaining ewe, now on her own, deciding to make her own way down the road following the central white lines. Hoping against hope that there were no other vehicles converging on the incident, Derek made chase, trying to run on the side of the animal, in the hopes of passing the sheep and cutting off her path so that he could return her to the van. A very surprised driver, in a car coming the opposite way, flashed past the sight of a sheep being chased by an irate farmer with his arms waving above his head trying to alert the oncoming traffic to the situation. The other driver was hot in pursuit as well, but, by now, had fallen behind. Just as Derek drew alongside the sheep, she spied an open gate into a front garden on her left-hand side and darted in quickly to avoid capture.

Realizing what she was doing, Derek stopped and turned to follow, only to meet head-on with the man who was frantically trying to keep up with him. Having sorted themselves out, they both entered the garden. By now Derek's patience was wearing very thin. Seeing that the sheep had stopped to eat the grass on the lawn, Derek was adamant that his last effort would not fail; he lunged forward onto the sheep with such a force that the sheep's legs buckled, causing Derek to do a somersault and land with the sheep on top of him, holding on to it with all his might.

At this precise moment the sensor light attached to the house came on, and three very confused people looked out on to their lawn to see the strange sight of Derek, with a sheep on top of him, telling the other driver: 'It may not look like it, but I've got it!' Relieved that the situation had been resolved, after Derek had thanked him he returned to his car and continued on his way. Derek was left to drag the sheep quite some considerable distance back to the van – and anyone who knows sheep will know how helpful they can be, by digging their feet into the ground and anchoring their legs to make life as difficult as possible. On reaching home. Derek collapsed into a chair, and we could tell from his sweaty red face and the bramble leaves stuck in his hair that the pick-up had not gone smoothly.

Mandy always enjoys working with the sheep and is very good

with them. She came to us straight from school to work as an animal care assistant in 1986; she has gained considerable experience over the years and now acts as supervisor. She has shared my interest in wildlife and attended many lectures and care seminars with me to widen her knowledge. Where my favourite animal must be the badger, her wildlife passion is the fox, but she has affection and consideration for all animals. Tall and dark-haired, we have seen her change from a teenager, through the 'gothic image', into a young woman and she is very much part of the farm.

She shares my grief when losing animals that have become friends. Sadly, our red setter came to the end of her life after fourteen years. We had both seen her change from a young, prancing dog to a very grey-muzzled old lady who eventually spent most of her life in the armchair in the kitchen, bemused by the comings and goings of an assortment of animals. It took a long time before we got used to the empty chair.

3

Birds, Bats and Bites

It was all the Council's fault!

In the village of East Huntspill, the Council decided to replace all the roof tiles on the council houses – this was in May. Lo and behold, as the tiles were taken off, nests of starlings were discovered. The workers that did not have the heart to kill them sent the baby birds down to us in an assortment of cardboard boxes. It was very difficult; many were so tiny that to rear them would be practically impossible. However, we adapted the incubator and did what we could to help them survive, more out of enthusiasm than experience as we had only just started looking after injured and orphaned animals and still had a great deal to learn. Placing each group in the lid of an egg box, lined with tissue, I soon got the hang of feeding the gaping mouths. This was always followed by the small fledgling turning round and placing its bottom over the edge of the box to give me a little package, in the same way as they would do with their parent bird, who would take the package of excreta and get rid of it away from the nest, keeping the bedding nice and clean.

Thoughts on diets change, and each species has its own require-ments, but at that time I was feeding them on dog food, bread and hard-boiled egg mashed together and the older ones thrived. I am afraid I did not have much success with the very tiny pink babies, but in general I think the trick is more a question of little and often than anything else. The older the fledglings became, the dirtier they were, and it was a question of continually changing the tissue in the boxes, every time there was a feed. We reached the stage of having eleven scruffy fledglings that should soon be feeding themselves.

At this time the cheese room was not being used, so we moved the boxes out of the house (even I sighed in relief) and put the birds in a larger cage upstairs. There were branches in the cage to get them used to perching and food trays on the bottom for them to feed from, although they seemed to walk through them more than anything else. Starlings are such greedy birds, they would squabble and fight over the food, getting themselves sticky all over. Gobbling up great mouthfuls, the mixture would ooze from the sides of their mouths and they would then decide to shake their heads vigorously so that the excess food flew from the sides of their beaks to stick in globules in all the surrounding areas. It really was a job and a half to keep them clean. They had accepted me as the parent bird, and while cleaning the cage, I had eleven squawking starlings up my arms, on my back and in my hair. It makes you wonder why I did not give up looking after the things there and then! Eventually the happy day came when it was time for them to leave – naturally, I mean, although other thoughts had crossed my mind!

It was a lovely warm day and, as the cage had been placed by the cheese room window, I opened the cage and the window and left the birds to decide if they wanted to take their first flight. Going down the wooden staircase, I closed the hatch to keep the cats away and left them to it. By lunchtime, five had gone and by late afternoon only one remained. After the milking, Derek and I had to deliver a bag of feed to a neighbour and we went out in the car, enjoying a short break from the farm.

I bet you're glad the starlings have gone,' said Derek.

'Mmm, yes, but I hope they will be all right. I certainly shan't miss cleaning up after them,' I replied.

Not being able to stay out too long as we have to shut the chickens up before it starts to get dark, we returned to give ourselves a chance to have a cup of tea before going about the shutting up. Turning into the yard, we laughed at the spectacle before us by the back door. On the mounting steps stood every one of those flipping starlings, and as I got out of the car, they all flew to meet me! It was just like the Alfred Hitchcock film *The Birds*. Walking back up the wooden staircase with my brood still attached to me and scolding each other, I settled them back in their cage. They did eventually fly away in the next few days, but every time we get baby starlings brought in, we always get the feeling of – Oh, no!

The prettiest fledglings I have reared must be little blue tits. They remind me of miniature penguins, as they rest their beaks on fluffed-up chests. Their call is very distinctive and is one that I can recognize around the farm, although I must admit that most other bird song defeats me apart from the obvious. Most birds take only three weeks from the time of hatching to leaving the nest, and the parents are kept very busy finding enough food to allow for this very quick growth.

Blue tits are unusual in the fact that they lay only one brood in a season, where other birds will have two or even three broods in a year. Their eggs are synchronized to hatch just as the glut of caterpillars appear, particularly the winter moth caterpillar. The female moth is unable to fly and lays her eggs on the bare branches or buds of trees, with a particular liking for apple, pear or oak trees. The eggs remain over winter on the trees and hatch out in the spring; the caterpillars are actually dispersed by the wind from one tree to another. Perhaps the fact of these eggs being laid in oak trees is why the blue tit very often will favour oak trees to nest in. They make their nest in a hole in the tree and will take up residence in a nest box quite happily, especially if it is fixed to an oak tree.

A lot of blue tits' nests are found in the dormouse boxes that are put out for survey work, but this is never minded as the young are up and gone before the dormouse thinks to use the boxes for breeding. In the Mendips, where roe deer can be found, almost all the blue tit nests will be lined with the tell-tale zigzag hairs of deer.

We have quite a variety of birds around the farm and they all have their special territories. Alongside the barn, which is now the Visitor Centre, there is a large horse-chestnut tree and some very old alder trees where you can frequently see tree-creepers going up and down the gnarled bark in search of food.

The motorway runs quite close to the farm now, a good thing as far as bringing visitors is concerned but there is a continual drone in the distance of traffic, which is not so good. The motorway came long before I did, but I would like to have seen it as it was many years ago with just a gently twisting road stretching between the two villages of East and West Huntspill. There are still a lot of withy trees lining the road but, Derek has told me, there used to be several magnificent elm trees in the area, sadly all victims of the Dutch elm disease.

We have a walk that the visitors can do which takes them past the local farms, many still owned by the family. Cousin Marcus has the farm opposite and, as you reach the River Brue, you can see Uncle Den's farm by the river. There are sluice gates by the river and here, if you are lucky, swans can be seen, and occasionally cormorants. In early summer the swallows skim the water to drink and to catch the surface insects that can be found in great numbers on very hot days. The mud on the riverside is taken to mould into saucer-shaped nests in buildings, and there are many repeated flights as they flash through open doorways or broken windows, building the nest up little by little.

We used to have several swallows' nests on the farm during the summer. One year the flies were biting at the cows' legs and making them very fidgety while being milked, and Derek decided to spray the cows with a special repellent which kept the flies off the cows for a month. We did it for three months, just when the flies were at their worst in the middle of the summer, and it really worked. The cows were much quieter. The next year, we had no swallows' nests on the farm at all. The food supply of flies that would hover over the herd waiting to be milked had gone, and without realizing it, we had affected the swallows. It was six years before the swallows returned to us.

Derek, when he has been over by the river checking the cattle in the evening, has watched Daubenton's bats darting over the surface of the river taking over the nighttime shift in this territory, looking for insects and even small fish occasionally as dusk begins to fall.

The walk crosses a field and carries on down an old drove called Wooley Beggar Lane, which is really only a track. Very often long-tailed tits seem to live in a family along here and small groups move swiftly through the hedgerow, perching briefly before setting off again. Meandering through the perimeters of the flat fields, the track winds up to the road which then crosses the motorway. Although the M5 mars the landscape, the motorway bridge affords a good view of the basin of flat land which is part of the Levels and moors to be found in Somerset.

It is an area that many travel past and would consider uninteresting, unless they took the time to turn away from the busy roads and discover the very slow way of life that has not changed for many years, especially on the peat moors. Here farmers can still be found milking cows out in the fields during the summer using milking bails, as many fields are too far away from the farms for the cows to be taken back and forth for milking. A bail is a portable milking unit that can be transported by tractor, sited in the field where the cows are grazing, and used to milk the cows out in the open air; the milk is then transported back to the farm after each milking in a portable bulk tank. Peat is extracted from the moors, and areas that are no longer in use have been flooded to create natural habitat. The Somerset Trust for Nature Conservation has a reserve at Westhay which has colonized quickly and has a wealth of variety in wildlife species. Even the otter can be found on the moors. Withies are grown for basket-making and old country crafts still survive. It is an area of great natural beauty.

Continuing down from the motorway bridge, our walk follows a little-used road to make its final way back to the farm. Moorhens, caught unawares, dive for cover. Their huge green feet belie how adept the bird is at swimming, wading or even climbing trees. If you are lucky, you might see a heron standing silently in the rhine, a very efficient fisherman who will often catch quite big eels. We have a heronry near us and there are not many days that you do not see one somewhere in the rhines along our road. Many people do not realize that such a big bird can be found in the wild, and we have even had visitors return from the walk and come to tell us that one of our herons has escaped and is standing like a sentry in a rhine a little way further down the road!

Many people bring birds in to us, but once it was eggs. After the flood disaster in our area in 1981, a new sea wall was being built to contain the high tides. A local contractor, Arthur Duckett, with very large American-style lorries, brought in the rubble and was involved with the building of the sea defences. He was very concerned, one wet and windy day, to see that an oyster-catcher had settled on part of the development and laid two eggs. Arthur realized that the eggs would be protected by law but he could not hold up the building work for the sake of an oyster-catcher. Contacting the Department of the Environment, he obtained a licence to remove the eggs and brought them out to me to see if I could incubate them. As luck would have it the incubator was running anyway, so I popped them in and did not really think much more about it.

Eventually some of the bantam chicks hatched out and, to our surprise, in amongst them sat a very pretty fluffy brown and white chick with a long beak. The other oyster-catcher egg did not hatch so we only had the one. Luckily, oyster-catcher chicks are nidifugous which means that they hatch with down, can see, are able to run and can usually feed themselves. This is the case with waders and ducks. For birds born blind, naked and totally reliant on their parents, the name is nidicolous. (How's that for blinding you with science!) He sat quite happily amongst his chirping mates, and we were lucky to have the chicks at the same time as they were able to teach him how to peck and find his food. If you get one chick on its own, you can sometimes get it to feed by tapping a pair of tweezers in a dish where the food is, to mimic a parent teaching them. With his huge feet he was soon at least two inches taller than his mates but no one seemed to mind and they all got on well. We supplemented his food with maggots, dog meat and sometimes fish as his normal diet would be shellfish.

He was nicknamed Ollie. Both the bantams and Ollie grew big enough to be put in the outside pens that we have running alongside the haybarn. It was thought that he would take off and find others of his own kind when he was ready – the estuary is not far from here as the crow (or oyster-catcher) flies. I was lucky enough to see him go. It was just as evening was falling and I was the one doing the shutting up of poultry pens. Ollie tried his wings and then lifted off. The sun was just setting, and it was a lovely sight as he soared past the farm building, down the homeground and over our neighbour Michael's farm. Going back in the house, I told Derek that at last 'Ollie' had flown away.

But the next day Ollie was back! Michael had found him pecking around in the haybarn and returned him to us. He flew away again a couple of weeks later, only to be found walking down the middle of the High Street in Burnham-on-Sea, and was taken to the RSPCA Wildlife Unit. Colin Seddon, who works at the Unit, rang and said that he thought he had our Ollie, as when the bird was taken in, he recognized a tin of dog food as soon as the staff went in to feed him! He obviously needed some time with his own kind so Ollie was kept in a pen down there with other oyster-catchers for a while, and was eventually released on Steart Island where many oyster-catchers are found.

It is surprising what is inborn in an animal or bird, and what sometimes has to be taught. We were discussing this at a lecture that Doug Woods, a retired butcher with a limitless knowledge of wildlife, was giving in Bristol. He told us how the heron and the swift desert their young when they are ready to become self-sufficient; the young heron will first have to learn to fly from the nest and find water, and then it will have to teach itself how to fish and catch its own food. Even more incredible is the swift. From the time that a young swift leaves its nest for its first flight it will remain on the wing for at least two years without ever touching the ground. It will feed on the wing, sleep, preen and even mate. Once fit, the swift must find its own way to Africa, returning the following year even though it is still too young to breed. It will not be until the second year that the swift will nest and for the first time will land after its continuous flight. It is estimated that in their lifetime of ten years or more, they will fly over a million miles. Isn't nature wonderful?

Newspapers are very often looking for animal stories, and on one occasion when they contacted us for a story we happened to have a baby robin and a pipistrelle bat in at the same time. The headlines read 'Batman and Robin at New Road Farm'! Bats are very difficult to rear. All that we know on feeding them has come from Cheri Vincent, who has cared for all kinds of bats over the years. We have only had pipistrelle bats brought into us, but Somerset can boast fifteen species of bat that can be found in the county due to its ancient woodland and caves. Baby bats we have fed with goat's milk, but once they wean the difficulties start. A pipistrelle bat only weighs the same as three 20p pieces or ten paper clips, and when you think that that contains everything, all its organs, wings and that superb sonar system, it is really quite incredible.

We have bats that come to the farm in the evening, but only in small numbers, so instead of having a roost here, I think we are just part of their feeding ground. A bat will eat between two and three thousand insects in one night. Small midges will be eaten whilst the bat is still in flight, but if a moth is taken then the bat will roost and eat it in a favourite place and food remains will accumulate on the ground below. It is therefore very difficult to replace this diet, but it has been found that they will eat mealworms. This is where the dedication comes in because what you do is this: pinch off the head of the mealworm and then squeeze the body out like a tube of toothpaste. The bat will eat it as the substance oozes out. Particularly with bats, I like to show them when I am feeding

. . . poor bat standing next to a mountain of mealworms . . .

them to make people realize they are not as horrible as they would believe.

Being so tiny, bats can squeeze into almost any small hole that may appear in the flashing of a roof or by a loose tile. The thought of bats always conjures up pictures of cobwebs and old draughty buildings, but they really prefer warm modern houses – many people unknowingly have unpaying tenants in their roofs. Because pipistrelle bats can live in colonies of up to a thousand in a roost it is important for them to feel close to another body, so I either give them a hot water bottle next to some cloth for them to hang on to, or literally wear them because they will hang quite happily from your jumper. I was showing one to the visitors and also feeding it, and was explaining the reason why we feed them on mealworms, usually eleven or twelve a day, in order to replace the thousands of insects that they would catch on the wing. But I really could not have explained myself clearly enough. As the crowd moved away, one of the ladies watching turned to her friend and said: 'Isn't that amazing, you would not think that a little thing like that would have the strength to squeeze out two to three thousand mealworms in one night!' I had the mental vision of the poor bat standing next to a mountain of mealworms, trying to iron each tube out one by one with its wings. I did not spoil her illusion.

Bats are protected by law and, when found in attics, one must remember the good that they do. Think of all those midges that would be bothering you if the bats were not there. As with many creatures their habitats are being lost and we humans have done a great deal of damage, many times unwittingly by spraying timbers against woodworm using fluids that have the power to kill bats for up to ten years after application, and sometimes by filling cavity walls. If you are thinking of doing any alteration and have the slightest of suspicions that bats may be present, then contact English Nature who will advise you and usually ask a member of a bat group to call and see you. There are fluids that can be used against woodworm that do not harm bats, and ways round problems that can be beneficial to both you and the bats. However, I am afraid the one thing that kills bats more than anything is the dear little cat.

Our cats are very good and seem to know that anything brought into the house is not 'food'. Perhaps too good at times, because we find it necessary to have a pest control contract with the council as with all our old buildings we would be unable to keep the numbers of mice and rats down properly. Our 'rat-man' is Jim and he is one of life's characters, a man it is always a pleasure to see. He arrives in his yellow council van, which he strategically places out of sight when we are open so that people will not realize why he is here, and with his pot of poison, melts into the background going quietly about his job. A special kind of bait is used on our farm because of the many birds and animals that we have here. As he slipped through the yard one day he encountered a crowd of children who had just arrived; hiding his bucket behind his back, he casually pretended to be looking at the plants, but one of the children had seen him before. 'Hello, Mr Rat-man,' shouted one child, quite proud that he had recognized him. Sixty-five pairs of eyes turned to his direction. Weakly smiling, he waved and continued on his way, his 'cover' blown.

Pigeon control was part of Jim's job. Where pigeons have become a problem, they are caught and destroyed. Someone objected to this, and could not understand why they could not be released somewhere else. Annoyed that his knowledge was being questioned, and to prove a point, Jim trapped and marked some birds early one morning. 'I kept them in my little van all day,' he said, 'all round the country lanes, all round Wookey, up and over the Mendips, I tell you 'twas a wonder they weren't dizzy, and I finally let them go right over by Bristol. Do you know what? They were home before I was!' Point proved.

People do not always know very much about birds, and we had a call from someone who had found a baby sparrowhawk in their garden. Not knowing how to look after it, they wondered if we would go and collect it. At that time my nephew Lincoln and his girlfriend Liz were staying at the farm. They came for a working holiday, having travelled from Kent. Lincoln did some much needed building repairs and Liz kept herself busy in the garden. Both had been fascinated at the variety of animals and birds that arrive at our doorstep and when I said that I had to go and pick this bird up, they asked if they could come with me. Lincoln, who was in his early twenties, had taken after his father and was very tall, being at least 6 foot 7 inches in height; and being very slim he had to fold himself to get into the car. The weather was hot and we had the windows of the car open. Lincoln's long hair (which would be the envy of any girl) was blowing with the breeze and we were teasing him about it spoiling his hair-do! Trying to change the subject, he explained that he had always been interested in birds of prey and was looking forward to seeing the fledgling. It may not be a sparrowhawk, I warned him, not everyone knows one bird from another. At least they had it in a container so we had not bothered to bring a box.

When we pulled up outside the house, I left Lincoln to fetch the bird as I turned the car round and Liz and I sat expectantly waiting for Lincoln's return. At last the front door opened, with the lady thanking Lincoln for looking after the fledgling for her. Lincoln was gently carrying an ice-cream container which was covered with a cloth. As he got into the car, we waited for the result. 'Are you ready for this?' he said with a smile. He lifted the cloth carefully: there, proud as punch on a nice clean towel, sat a baby goldfinch!

Birds of prey are looked upon with awe, but the poor old magpie is considered to be just a pest. Their numbers have indeed increased, but it has now been proved that they do less damage in preying on the eggs and young of small bird species than the kestrel or sparrowhawk, all of which at one time were heavily controlled by gamekeepers. There has been a sharp decline in some of our more common species such as the wren, the robin and the blackbird, but this is thought to have more to do with the climate of recent years, coupled with intensive farming which does not allow weeds, which in turn do not give seeds, nor attract insects. But this balance is hopefully being redressed as we are all becoming aware of the need for conservation. So don't blame the magpie, it's not all his fault.

Derek has had to do more than his fair share when it comes

to running around collecting things and, as we live near the sea, he often has to pick up seagulls. He thought no more of it when a call came through asking him to go to Weston-super-Mare to collect a seabird. On his way out to the car Derek was interrupted by a visitor asking about some of the animals, and once he had finished talking, he went off without the carry box and any catching equipment. When he arrived at the scene, which was the Helicopter Museum, he found that his client, wasn't a seagull at all; in fact it was a gannet, the largest and the most spectacular breed of seabirds. It was really quite impressive to look at but exceedingly difficult to catch! Gannets, if blown off course, will land and are unable to take off again unless they are on a cliff. Unable to fly, this one was making the most of its seven-foot wing-span to gain speed if nothing else. Having commandeered extra help the situation should have been under control, but all the helpers were wary of the strong beak that was being wielded at every opportunity. Derek eventually cornered the bird to the applause of the crowd of spectators that by this time had gathered, and using begged and borrowed bits and pieces, quickly tied cardboard round the bird's body and put a soft cloth money-bag over its head to quieten it down. The power of the bird, Derek said, was quite incredible and the plumage was so attractive. The bird must have been at least four years old as they do not get their full plumage until then. They do not have any nostrils on the outside of their beaks and this allows them to dive from anything up to 100 feet head-first into the sea, which means that they hit the water at around 60 miles per hour. Derek took this bird straight to the Wildlife Unit as they have the proper facilities for seabirds.

Despite the time taken up on these call-outs, it is always interesting to see these birds, which in our lifestyle we do not have the chance to see very often. Little auks, snipe, a fulmar and sandpipers are some of the more unusual ones that Derek has collected at different times.

The fulmar Mandy remembers, as it was she who had to care for it until it was sent down to the RSPCA Unit. It is similar in looks to a gull but has the distinctive feature of two nostril tubes which are prominently placed on its hooked beak. From these it is able to eject a dark, foul-smelling liquid as a type of defence, and which is very difficult to get rid of. It was not until Mandy had been thoroughly doused in this liquid that she realized it had this little habit and the bird was quickly placed in a pen so that Mandy could come and voice her disgust to us. I'm afraid that with our sense of humour, there wasn't a great deal of sympathy shown! Fulmar can be found on most of our coastline where the cliffs are suitable, and are one of our longest-living birds as they can attain the age of forty years. We were quite happy to keep one just for two days!

When dealing with birds that have large beaks, you must be very careful as they can do severe damage; indeed when handling them, I usually pop a rubber band over the beak. I received a telephone call from a local man stating that he had an injured heron. Could I possibly take it in? 'What injuries does it have?' I asked.

'Oh, it's been shot,' replied the local.

Puzzled, I asked if he knew how. Rather sheepishly, he admitted that he had shot it. The heron had been regularly stealing goldfish from his pond every morning – right in front of him, every day at breakfast time, and he had had enough. He reached for his gun and meant to shoot over its head to frighten it away, in the hope that it would not return. Unfortunately it moved, and to his mortification, he had shot it in the neck.

'Bring it down,' I said, 'and we will see to it.'

'Thanks ever so much, I'm on my way'; and the relieved local put the phone down. (He will remain anonymous for obvious reasons!)

I suddenly remembered that I had not warned him to watch the beak, but thought that he would be all right. He was used to handling animals and one usually masters the art of avoiding retaliation. A few minutes later, the car pulled into the yard. The heron had arrived (it eventually made a full recovery and was released). As I walked out to the car, the local got out to meet me. A nasty cut down one side of his nose and a completely smashed lens of his glasses told me that maybe I should have remembered to warn him. If he hadn't worn glasses, he could well have lost an eye.

'Got his own back, did he?' I asked. Like Queen Victoria – he was not amused!

4

My Badgers: Three Striped Heads and a Duke

'What now?' was my immediate thought, as one of my staff carried a cardboard box towards me. In the five years since Derek and I had turned our small dairy farm into an 'open farm', our reputation for looking after animals had grown and in its wake followed a great variety of creatures brought to our door for one reason or another. Certainly the noise coming from the box was not one that I recognized, a sort of mixture between a goose cackling and a dog barking. It was with some curiosity that I peered into the box to see three small grey forms, each no more than eight inches in length. Their coats were like velvet and each foot had five shiny even claws. Milky eyes looked up at me, from three small black and white striped heads, as I took my first look at three baby badgers that were to become very much part of my life over the next few months.

I had never seen badger cubs before. Most are born in January or February. Totally dependent on their mothers until eight to ten weeks of age, if orphaned they would normally remain underground and would die from starvation. These three had been brought in by building contractors laying drainage pipes, whose machinery went into the sett before they realized it was there. The mother was found dead with the three cubs still suckling her. Lost for what to do, one of the workmen remembered us, and they were quickly despatched to the farm. I could see that they were healthy and well fed but cold and whimpering so, as was the usual procedure for all patients, it was into the farmhouse kitchen and they were put by the Rayburn for warmth – but only *after* a quick dusting to get rid of the not-so-attractive fleas that were running through their coats! The warmth soon began to work and three sleepy badgers were quiet for a while, giving us time to gain advice from knowledgeable friends and much-used reference books.

Fascinated, I watched as they entwined their bodies, snuggling for comfort. They must have been only about five weeks old as their eyes had only just opened and as yet could not focus properly. When hunger eventually disturbed them, I found it easier to use a syringe to feed them as they were so tiny. First, though, it was necessary for each cub in turn to be wiped between the back legs with a warm wet cloth to simulate the feel of the mother licking them. This made them empty their bowels and bladder, by which time they were keen to feed. Taking each one in turn, I found that there were two female cubs and one male, and they were duly named – the two girls were called Bluebell and Primrose, and the boy was named Willow. With three cubs to see to and the routine of cleaning as well as feeding, it took nearly an hour to sort everything out. As this had to be repeated every four hours my days became very full: I started at six in the morning, and the last feed was at midnight. We moved the cubs into a box in the living room with a heated pad to keep them warm; this meant we could keep an eye on them all the time. As I fed each cub in turn, they would lie on my lap when full or snuggle beside me in the chair and I was accepted as Mum. I don't know who was more content, them or me; to be so close and to be trusted by such beautiful animals was my privilege.

There was a slight musky smell to the cubs, particularly when first picked up and when excited, ready for their food, and this is what would form their family smell. Each badger has a musking gland at the base of its tail, and within their own family group they will constantly musk against each other. This forms a family scent by which each badger can identify a member of its own family, and they would all certainly know if a badger was from another area. Seeing as the badger's sense of smell is 500 times as strong as ours, this is quite an easy way for them to find out who is friend or foe.

Sitting quietly late one evening by the log fire, with the three cubs sleeping soundly on my lap, I began to realize just how difficult it was going to be to release them even if I managed to rear them. They would have no family group to return to nor a territory that would belong to them. Pushing these worries to the back of my mind, I concentrated on the present and decided to take each problem as it came. Certainly, I can remember thinking that I was the lucky one, sitting there watching the flames in the fire – for it was early March, lambing time for us, and Derek was outside in the cold bitter air making the last check on the sheep before we went to bed. Moving to the window, I looked out over the farmyard; the moon was shining so brightly there was no need for lights, and the glistening frost gave detail even to the spiders' webs draped over the hedgerow. Out there all over the country, many, many badger cubs deep in their setts were being nursed by the sow badgers, oblivious to the cold weather and the cruel outside world. Given another four or five weeks, spring would be on its way and then it would be time to venture above ground for the first time and experience the new smells and sights, completely different from their life underground. They would stay close to their mother, as she taught them about their territory, where to forage, which paths to take, and the art of mutual grooming and play. She would also introduce them to the rest of the family and protect them. Goodness, I thought, how on earth was I going to try and do the same?

It was less than a week before the cubs progressed to drinking from the bottle and already, when placed on the ground, they would endeavour to move around, albeit very shakily. Their eyes were beginning to focus although normally they would not need them underground, relying mainly on their sense of smell.

As you can imagine, the cubs caused a lot of interest with friends; one friend in particular, Ken Chapman, a keen photography enthusiast, offered to take pictures of the cubs during their growing-up period. It was during their first 'session', three weeks after their arrival, that I noticed that Willow seemed lethargic even though he was still taking his food as normal. His eyes were still bright, and as there were no other outward signs, I did not worry too much. It was a warning sign I should have reacted to straight away, but I did not realize its importance. I awoke the next morning to find him dead. The feeling of failure was tremendous, and I immediately doubted my ability to rear the other two successfully. We took his little body to the vet's to have a post mortem carried out. I was sure it was something I had done wrong in the rearing. In a way it was. Willow had died from a lung infection. When bottle-feeding any animal it is important not to let it drink too fast as liquid can overflow into the lungs. This can cause an infection, which is very difficult to rectify, even with antibiotics, in one so small. Wildlife has the ability to bear infection and injury without showing outward signs until the condition has become very serious, a lesson I have learnt and remembered ever since.

Disheartened by my failure, I continued rearing 'my girls', only now with some slight apprehension. My affinity with those badger cubs had become so important to me that I could never have given them to someone else to rear, but the fear of making a mistake again was ever in my mind. I needed to know more about badgers, their lifestyle, social behaviour and environment, and the only way I could do that was to read some books! Word soon got around that we were rearing badger cubs, and people who belonged to local badger groups visited to see them, so my knowledge increased by listening to their experience.

Fate works in funny ways. Six days after Willow died, a local farmer, who had heard about our cubs, arrived at the farm one morning to see me. They had found a dead sow badger in the road outside their farm. Later that morning they had been moving some silage bags to feed their cows, and the farmer had discovered, tucked in a corner behind the bags, a single male badger cub that had been left there by his mother. Young sows will very often move away from the main sett to have cubs; this is because the dominant sow will have her cubs at the sett and there is a risk she may kill the cubs from another sow. The farmer, not sure if the dead sow had been the mother, had left the cub in the hope that the mother would return, although this was unlikely as they had disturbed the area so much. Unfortunately she had not, and by now the little cub was feeling cold and hungry. I took him into the house and Willow II joined the fold. I could see he was smaller than the girls; he was probably about two weeks younger as they were now nearly two months old.

Over the next few days I think I discovered why his mother left him! Never had I had anything so difficult to feed. After placing the teat from the bottle in his mouth I had to move the teat around, squeeze it, and cajole him into drinking. Then he would latch on to the teat and refuse to drink for a full ten minutes, after which he would suck as if he had not drunk all day. This is a problem that can often arise with badger cubs, possibly when the milk is not in plentiful supply. When the cub finds a teat that is full he will clamp on to it to prevent any other cub getting to it. When hand-rearing, all you can do is wait patiently until the cub relaxes. Once it realizes there is no competition, it will feed quite happily. Such an easy thing to say, but when two cubs have already wolfed their milk, dinner's going to be late and there are other jobs that need to be done, it is a great effort to act relaxed and happy when given this eyeball-to-eyeball confrontation from this arched stubborn body. He did grow out of this phase after a few days, but it was a sign of the stubborn personality that this young man had – and there were to be a few clashes later too!

We were told when our cubs arrived that, because we were hand-rearing them, their hair would fall out approximately two weeks after we had them. This is just a dietary upset, causing the hair to break at the base, and it soon regrows. However, this never happened with the girls. Maybe they were so young they did not notice the change in the diet, but poor Willow II was true to form and over the next few weeks, one by one, his hairs began to fall out. Apart from his definite striped black and white head, we had a totally bald baby badger on our hands. He was perfectly healthy and joined in as much as he could playing with the girls, who by now were full of mischief, but badgers play by getting hold of a fold of skin and tugging, so for him, at times, it proved rather painful.

They were not sleeping so much now and needed to play and explore. As they were still in the house, things were getting rather chaotic. With the sense of smell that badgers have, they know just what is behind the fridge door and exactly where the biscuit barrel is kept behind which cupboard door. All they have to do is find a way of opening doors. By the time you are a teenage badger those lovely long claws, so essential for digging, gleam from your front paws. Carefully placed, just in that small crevice between the cupboard and door, and hey presto, the door comes open. Even better, as most parents who have two young sons around the house would know, it takes years before children realize that doors are for closing, and who can blame a poor innocent badger cub, passing by an open door, for just taking a look inside. It has to be seen to be believed as to what five packets of breakfast cereals tossed around the house can look like! Maybe, if I caught them in action, I could have been cross, but on discovery of their latest escapade, finding three exhausted cubs curled up together with sugar puffs stuck to every part of their anatomy, I'm afraid any anger melted away to laughter. With plenty of toys, not too much damage was done, but it was decided that it was now best to keep them under a watchful eye. So during the day they were moved into reception where either I or Jean, our secretary, would be on duty. Being on the farm, most of our staff wear jeans and trainers; and a sure sign of having been in the office was someone walking about with wet chewed laces trailing from their feet. It must be something to do with worms being part of their staple diet in the wild that attracted the cubs to laces!

The girls were easily weaned by the end of April, happily going on to creamed rice and then literally anything. Willow was not ready to wean yet and, being the youngest, he was spoilt. He always was a little bit of a wimp. When the girls got a bit too boisterous, he could put the 'poor little me' look on his face and cower behind your legs only to be picked up and gloat, because that was exactly what he wanted you to do.

It was becoming increasingly difficult to contain the girls without the house being completely destroyed, so we decided to build a temporary sett out of straw bales in an old part of the cowshed. Willow was with them during the day and came in the house at night, as he was still not weaned and his new coat not yet coming through. He commandeered the airing cupboard which was nice and warm, only coming out when he wanted his bottle or was searching for Barney, our family dog, for company and someone to play with. Indeed, he built up quite a relationship with Barney and they remained good friends all the time Willow stayed here.

The temporary pen had plenty of space but I had to keep up my contact with the cubs by having at least three playtimes through the day for around half an hour, when everyone was fair game. The badger is of the same family as the ferret but is a much larger animal. The dentition and power in the jaws of the badger are such that it can actually amputate fingers so, even in play, it can be a painful exercise. My arms and legs were black and blue from the games of nip and run, because as 'surrogate mum' I was as fair game as anyone. In the front of the pen we put a very high metal sheeted gate as there was a slight worry that local badgers might object to the cubs being on their territory and might try and get in to kill them. Badgers are very territorial. They have a special area around their home which they mark out with dung pits around the perimeter to warn other badgers not to trespass. When the RSPCA's Wildlife Centre near us has injured badgers in its pens the animals mark against the fences, and the local badgers in turn come up to the other side of the fence and dung along the outside, warning them that they are on their territory. I have since heard this from other people caring temporarily for sick or injured badgers (colourfully described as the 'Battle of the Shits'!). We, in fact, have never had any problems with marking against our badgers, which is very surprising as we have a very old sett two fields away from us, but I wonder if, as the cubs came from only a couple of miles away, they might have been from the same social group.

It was at this time that we were asked if we would take the cubs up to London to the Food and Farming Exhibition to be held in Hyde Park in early May. The Exhibition was to mark the 150th anniversary of the Royal Agricultural Society of England and the Centenary of the Ministry of Agriculture, Fisheries and Food. Besides many other displays, each area group of the National Farmers' Union was to represent the farmers and give an insight into the food that is produced and the work that is put into the rural community. We have done several shows before, and on these occasions take animals that we know will not be stressed by the extra attention of the general public. The badgers, at this stage, did not care where they were as long as they were with me, so, confirming that we could sleep in the marquee together with the animals, we agreed to go, taking other animals with us as well to create a 'Wildlife and Country' display. Willow was still not weaned, and I felt the problem of bottle-feeding would be too complicated, so we decided just to take the girls. Jean, our secretary, who was very fond of Willow, said she would take him home with her for the three days. (She had no idea what she was committing herself to!) Simon, my youngest son, who had on many occasions helped me with the badgers, came as well. Our cousin Clive was doing a sheep-shearing exhibition in the same marquee, so we all travelled up to London together in a jeep with animals, feed and equipment in a trailer behind, stopping occasionally to check on everyone and make sure that all was well.

As my parents came from the London area I had visited London on many occasions, and Simon knew well the delights of the London Underground where 'you can buy a ticket and go round and round all day, as long as you don't come up'! Clive had very rarely been to London and certainly never driven in London before. The drive up the motorway and the ease of following the signs for Central London lulled him into a false sense of security. He could not understand all the fuss that people made of driving in London until we reached the top of the road, and being typically in the wrong lane we caught sight of Hyde Park – all we had to do was cross four lanes of endless traffic going north and join the four-lane road going south, getting on the nearside lane within 50 yards as there was our entrance, and I knew from bitter experience that once you pass a road you are looking for, you rarely see it again because all this business of 'All I have to do is go round to the left and we shall be back where we want' never works. Clive looked at me and said 'Now what do I do?!' Looking totally confident, I told him to wind his window down, stick out his arm to indicate right, and go. Clive, who is a super character, being larger than life both in build and in personality, did just that. The jeep and trailer turned safely into the entrance despite noisy objections from other vehicles and digital instructions.

This was one of the largest shows I had ever been to. High security fences totally surrounded the show area and uniformed guards checked passes and veterinary reports to prove the animals were healthy before you were allowed in. It was also necessary to report to the resident veterinary personnel on arrival so that they knew that the animals were in residence. We checked our map to find the location of our marquee – not an easy task in the sea of white tents, show rings, stalls and attractions – but eventually we arrived, quickly unpacked and set up the pens for the animals. Any reservations I had about bringing the badger cubs were soon dispelled as they frolicked in their new pen, working off their energy after the journey.

Having got the animals settled, it was our turn to find our quarters. The marquee was huge, covering the many stands displaying the wares of Somerset. Cheeses, cider, wine and basket-making were only a few of the varied products that Somerset can boast. At the bottom of the marquee was a stage with seating for approximately 150; here was where an entertainments programme would run throughout the three-day event, where visitors would listen to a local folk group called the Yetties, join in competitions, watch spinning and, of course, Clive's sheep-shearing demonstration. A tent was added to the middle of the marquee to take the animals. We were placed on the side, then there was a pen with calves, and

The author, with Willow (the first), Primrose and Bluebell

The three cubs at five weeks old

Bottle feeding

Bluebell and Primrose feeling very relaxed

Badgers in a basket, Bluebell and Primrose

Bluebell with Bracken and adopted cub Thistle

Fun at feeding time for Thistle and Bluebell

Sage, the beautiful barn owl

Orphaned field vole being fed with a paintbrush

One of a family of orphaned baby dormice, just as big as a fingertip

Orphan fox cub suffering from dehydration, eventually nursed back to health

Fox cub Heidi

another pen with some large black pigs. People everywhere busied themselves with the last-minute preparations for the first day, the most important one as the Queen and the Duke of Edinburgh were to visit that day. Others who were finished sauntered over to see the cubs and admire the stand.

As yet we had not found our quarters, nor seen any sight of an area suitable for retiring. Enquiries to fellow exhibitors proved fruitless and apprehension set in. All was resolved when the security officer in charge of our marquee came and asked who were the poor souls sleeping in the tent. Owning up, I quickly stated that I hoped it was near the animals. 'Right beside you, Ma'am', he said with a smile, and we all turned and looked at the large black pigs. No, we weren't actually in with them, but an area was curtained off by the side of them and I can remember, as I snuggled down into my sleeping bag, that the smell was not *too* bad – but then again, we did have three more days to go!

'Poor souls' was the right description because, arising at 5.30 the next morning, it made no difference that we had come up from the country or that we were farmers born and bred – it was still absolutely freezing. Muffled with every item of clothing I could muster, I went in search of the kettle in the portakabin belonging to the security officer, who had kindly said we could use it. All our animals were sound asleep except for Sage, the barn owl, who enjoyed this time of day, head bobbing at the glitter and colour of all the furnishings on the stands. Scrabbling out from the canvas, I stood to see London with the sun rising behind the trees. My breath freezing in the cold morning air showed me the reason for my sleeplessness. But even at this hour traffic filled the roads and neon lights flickered to catch your attention: London never sleeps, as I was to find out later that evening. It all seemed so alien. On the one hand London was carrying on in its usual way, but even as I stood there with the early morning sun shimmering on the Serpentine, I could already hear the drone of the portable milking machines going into action – even shows cannot stop the need for milking twice a day. The morning chorus was under way, competing with the sound of the traffic together with the lowing of cattle and bleating of sheep; just for three days, two worlds were going to join.

By the time I found the kettle, I wasn't the first in the queue – Clive had beaten me to it, his only problem being that he does not *need* very much sleep. Jovial as ever, it was a good start to the day.

The badger cubs tumbled out for their breakfast of weetabix which was followed by the usual playtime. We had arranged the pens so that when the animals were tired or fed up with all the attention they could go into a chamber behind the straw bales and sleep undisturbed. After having fed, cleaned and exercised the animals, our thoughts were turning to our own rumbling stomachs and Simon was sent off in search of food. I hoped I did not smell too much of pigs as I changed ready for the show to begin. Hot dogs and onions were breakfast, the price of sending Simon for food, but none of us minded.

Certainly the weather was on our side, as the nippy morning was changing into what promised to be a lovely day. There was a special atmosphere and excitement as the gates opened to let the visitors in. We had organized it, Simon and I, that we would take it in turns to man the stall, which would also give us some freedom to go out and see the show ourselves. There was so much interest in the animals that it really did not work that way. So many people were asking questions there were times when we wished that we too had a chamber behind the straw to go and hide in! Many, many children as well as adults did not know what the badger cubs were and the most surprising number thought they were skunks. One very knowledgeable gentleman pointed them out to his wife: 'Cor, look over 'ere, Doris'; guiding her over to the stall, he nodded a greeting at me and said, 'My wife's never seen otters before.' Smiling back, I thought to myself 'and she still hasn't now', but they moved straight on, which was just as well, as he wasn't the type to correct (and he was bigger than me too).

People's mixed responses prove that it is a good thing we cannot all be alike. It was sad to hear the schoolchildren, who obviously knew so little about the countryside they rarely had the chance to visit (and that we take so much for granted). Both Simon and I got shouted at by a very irate lady who said we had no right to have these animals and they should be left in the wild. I tried to explain that, as orphans, they would not have survived and we had every intention of returning them to the wild, but she was not to be reasoned with. The most rewarding part was talking to people who realized how lucky they were to see a badger and discussing with them the dangers that now threaten our wildlife, mainly through human interference. Many farmers who were visiting the show stopped and chatted, several saying that they had badgers on their land but they would not tell other people about it. In general, farmers are protective of badgers, but foxes – well, that's another thing!

Just before midday, the marquee was cleared of the public to enable security to do a check as the Duke of Edinburgh was due to tour round the displays. While it was nice and quiet, we were able to get lunch sorted out for the badger cubs and the other animals. It also gave me the opportunity to phone back to home and check that all was well at the farm and with Willow. Everything was fine; Willow was feeding well and enjoying the company of four rough collies, and what with his nipping qualities, they were completely under his control and had given up all rights to the dog basket while he was in there!

When the Duke arrived at the marquee, he took the time to speak to as many people as he could. He asked Simon about the barn owl that we had with us and came over to see the badger cubs, also asking if they would be returned to the wild, which I was glad to be able to answer in the affirmative. Bluebell at that time was sitting on my lap with her two paws on my shoulders, nosing me in the face. 'Well, my girl,' I said to her after he had gone, 'there can't be many badgers who will be able to tell the tale in their sett in years to come, that they actually went up to London and met the Duke of Edinburgh.' Within twenty minutes the Duke and his entourage had swept out of the marquee and we were invaded once more. Clive had sheared several sheep throughout the day and the sound of the Yetties singing cider songs drifted through the tent. Several hot dogs later (I really must go and get the food myself next time), the afternoon was drawing to a close and the last visitors were meandering home. Time to exercise the badger cubs.

I had taken them out in the garden at home and found that they followed close to heel, so off Simon and I went with two cubs trotting behind, walking round by the perimeter of the security fences as this was where it was all grass. Stopping occasionally to snuffle around, they made sure that we were not too far away and would gambol towards us to catch up, sometimes following so closely that they were at times inadvertently given 'a lift forward' by getting in front of the foot instead of keeping behind. Badger cubs, when they emerge from the setts, follow close to their mother's feet, and sometimes, when unexpectedly come upon by people, the cubs can get confused in all the commotion of mother running back to the sett; and you do hear stories of people saying that the cubs have then mistakenly followed their feet, having lost contact with their own mother. What a sight it must have been, with Simon and I walking the cubs on one side of the railings, and the city men in their bowler hats with rolled-up umbrellas on the other side, making their way home after a day in the office.

Staggering back for their dinner, two exhausted badgers soon cleared up their food and settled for the night after a busy day; as yet they were not nocturnal, which made life a little bit easier at that time. Clive, like me, was beginning to crave some proper food and he managed to charm the security officer into looking after the animals for us during the night. He had such an amiable way about him that he seemed to be able to rustle up anything at any time. 'Don't worry,' said the security officer, 'I'm on till 6.30 a.m.' 'Goodness!' says I innocently, 'We shan't be that long.' Just something decent to eat and I shall be back to the sleeping bag – or so I thought.

Changed into fresh clothes (I'm sure I smell of pigs), Clive, Simon and I set off to explore London. Amazingly, we found a tube station almost immediately and despite a wonderful array of eating places so close to Hyde Park, we found ourselves entering the world of escalators and wind tunnels instead. Surfacing somehow after at least seven stations, we found ourselves at Trafalgar Square with the daunting statue of Nelson rising above the circling traffic, head and tail lights adding to the many neon lights, all so much brighter now darkness was falling. Pigeons lined the edges of the towering buildings, roosting for the night, their cooing still discernible above the city sounds. We wandered looking for a suitable place to eat. No, Simon didn't like Chinese . . . nor Indian . . . this one looks a bit expensive . . . I don't like the look of that one. This was not going to be as easy as I thought. Fifteen minutes later found the three of us sitting eating our dinner, Clive with a huge plate of food, Simon with a smile on his face and me thinking that when we have all finished, we shall be able to get out of McDonalds and go back to the showground. There is something about a polystyrene cup with a teabag and a string trailing from it that makes you think it would be nice to be home.

Clive suddenly remembered that some people he knew lived not very far away. They were friends who originally got to know his parents when they evacuated during the war, and they have continued to spend their summer holidays at the farm cottage each year. Well, thinks I, if they are in, we could leave Clive to socialize and Simon and I could return to the ever-attractive sleeping bags. Just as he promised, we found the house within half an hour and weren't we lucky, they were in. Welcoming us all, as only true Londoners can, they made us feel very much at home. They and their friends were just off out to a club but we were more than welcome to join them, no trouble at all; twenty minutes later we were dancing the night away – Simon included. One a.m. arrived and, despite a super evening, the sleeping bag loomed larger in my mind. People dwindled away and I chatted with Doug, one of Clive's friends, as we waited to make a move back to the showground. He was a taxi driver. We talked about living in London, and how although I often visited London and did the usual sightseeing there were still many areas I had never been to. This little lady was about to have her wishes made true!

By 2.15 a.m. we were packed in the back of his car and given the works. His knowledge of London was incredible, and I must admit it was all so interesting the image of the sleeping bag disappeared! The house where the Great Fire of London started, the roads named after the produce that was sold there hundreds of years ago – Pudding Lane, Fish Hill, Milk Street and many more. We toured the alleyways of Jack the Ripper Land in the East End of London, on to the Jewish area where many Polish and Russian Jews had settled around the time of the First World War. So many shops were obviously jewellers, the immigrants having brought their trade with them; and here, unbelievably, were bakers' shops with doors wide open and queues of people waiting to be served. It was now 3.30 a.m. and Doug parked the car so we could join the queue and taste the freshly baked Jewish bread. The smell of yeast filled the air and the garble of multilingual conversations fascinated us. Counters displayed vast choices of fillings, late suppers or early breakfasts, whatever – there was something to please everyone's taste. Totally another world from home where I knew the cats would be curled up on the rocking chair by the Rayburn, and out in the yard the cockerels would soon be crowing as dawn comes round once more. Tiredness overcame us when we had filled ourselves to the brim with the newly baked bread, and the last leg of the journey back to the showground was quiet. Thanking Doug for a very entertaining evening, we waved our goodbyes from our entrance and made our way back to the marquee. All were sound asleep as we checked on the pens before getting into the sleeping bags that I had thought of at so many different times through the night. I lay listening to the gentle snoring of our porky neighbours. I just knew that I must smell of pigs.

Clive, as I have said, does not *need* sleep and the dear man brought me a cup of coffee the next (or should I say, that same) morning at 6.30. As we still had plenty to do before the start of the day, it was not a minute too soon. Tiredness is a state of mind, I kept telling myself, and by the time the gates were open again there was no time to think about it. The day flew by and we repeated the walk in the evening with the cubs. Many of the exhibitors, now relaxing, had heard about the cubs and came over to chat, and we made several friends. We even found out that there was an exhibitors' cafeteria with decent food on site, so it was dinner and an early night. Clive went off to the night clubs! Tomorrow we go home, I comforted myself. I don't like to be away from home for long and Willow and the girls would be back together.

Even though the show finished earlier on the last day, doing all the packing up ready to go home was hard work. We took the badgers for their last walk in London to tire them out and, as expected, they slept all the way home. When we put them back in their pen, they made straight for their straw sett, curled up and went back to sleep. Probably just as happy to be home as I was.

Sitting having coffee in the kitchen after unpacking, I was to hear from Derek and Daniel, our other son, that their weekend had been eventful too. And there sitting by the fire, completely oblivious to all that was being said about him, was a bald badger with just a few wisps of his new coat coming through. Jean had taken him home on the Thursday as we left for London. Being Willow, as long as he knew that Jean was around he was completely at home. Jean's two sons, Simon and James, had a great game with him and, what with four large collies to play with as well, he was well and truly tired by bedtime. In the spare room opposite their bedroom, Jean had prepared a special bed made with blankets which he tossed around until it looked like a most uncomfortable heap. It was on top of this that he curled up and fell sound asleep, and not a peep was heard from him until the next morning. Waking up completely refreshed and confident, he decided after his early morning bottle that now was the time to show the collies who was boss, and he commandeered the dog basket. Any attempt to remove him from the basket was met with the kind of nip that only a badger cub can give, and the dogs decided to leave him to reign supreme. Even if he moved out, he kept one eye on the basket;

any signs of someone else moving in led to a show of acceleration which was unbelievable in such a small animal, and ended with a triumphant cub sitting square in the middle of the basket making it absolutely clear that he was not going to share!

Having got this situation under control, he decided it was time to find out what was behind the many cupboard doors that surrounded the kitchen. As we have said before, with a nose as keen as a badger's, you soon work out which doors are worth opening. The frequent sentence 'No, don't do that', which he seemed to be hearing rather a lot at that time, did not make any impression on a stubborn little badger like Willow. Jean was beginning to think that maybe she had made a mistake. By the time Keith, her husband, returned from work, Willow (and Jean) were tired out. Keith sat and had his tea, smiling at Willow sound asleep on his back with his paws twitching as he dreamed. 'Isn't he a good little chap?' he said. 'You', said Jean, 'haven't had him ALL day.' Halfway through the evening, Willow rolled out of the basket and found that Keith was prepared to play a game; and Jean, forgiving him for the day's events, joined in too.

Bedtime came and, once again, as good as gold, he settled on his untidy heap and was soon asleep, as was all the household. A few hours later, Willow awoke. If he had had a clock by the side of his

. . . triumphant cub sitting square in the middle of the basket . . .

bed, he would have known it was only 3.30 a.m., but this was only a minor detail. He really wasn't feeling very tired. Scenting with his nose in the air, he knew that Jean and Keith were sleeping not very far away. Perhaps they weren't tired either and would like another game. Padding quietly across the landing, he found himself by the side of the bed, which unfortunately was too high to scale. Jean had woken and heard the footsteps coming over to the bed, and so lay very still hoping he would go away again. Willow was not going to give up that easily; maybe if he whimpered and tugged at the bedclothes, he would get some response. Mistakenly, Jean supposed he was cold and lifted him on the bed, thinking he would snuggle down and go to sleep. A cold nose explored between the bedclothes. First he found some fingers that were waggled – he had been right, they would play! Further down the bed he even found some toes, and he soon learnt that if he nipped at parts of limbs they moved away quickly. I bet the game was to find them again! By this time not only Willow, but Jean and Keith were wide awake. They thought if they played with him for a while, he would soon get tired. Five o'clock found Willow just beginning to doze, and Keith making a cup of tea as he was to start work at half past six so it was hardly worth going back to sleep; and by this time he had also decided it was all Jean's fault for bringing that ***** badger cub home in the first place. For the sake of harmony and her marriage, Jean returned Willow to the farm on Saturday! Daniel and Derek between them had managed to look after Willow for the rest of the time, but I think he missed having me and the girls around the farm and pined for the last day until we got home. Derek does not like bottle-feeding at the best of times, and he found that Willow would try the patience of a saint.

Derek ruffled my hair. 'Glad to be home?' he asked. 'Very,' I answered with my hands cupped round my coffee. 'That's funny', said Derek, quizzically, 'I can smell pigs.' I must have a bath and wash my hair, I thought.

On return to our usual routine, the next task was to wean Willow. I'm not sure who became more frustrated. He obstinately decided he no longer wished to drink from a bottle but had not yet mastered the habit of eating without walking through his food, tipping it over or just sitting in it. Willow, whose second coat was now coming through, was not only prickly but also very sticky for a couple of days. My inspiration came one evening when cooking tea; I gave him a sausage which was taken to a corner with great interest, and little by little it was chewed, played with and finally eaten. After a week of sausages he was either heartily sick of them or just ready to go on to something else.

By now the badgers, at nearly five months of age, were eating cereals for breakfast and a meat and vegetable meal for lunch; in the evenings they had fruit and nuts, cheese, hardboiled eggs and sunflower seeds. Willow's favourite was bananas, although where he would have found them in the wild, I really don't know. The normal diet for badgers is 60 per cent earthworms, with the remainder made up of beetles and bugs, baby rabbits, carrion, mice and voles and even shoots, roots or fruits of plants, so they are true omnivores. There were quite a few times that September when I found myself completely badgerless after all three had disappeared into the hedgerow. As time passed, I became more ill at ease, as I wondered where they had got to. Eventually three black and white heads would return stained with blackberry juice all over their faces, and once I realized what they were up to, I no longer worried and would just walk on slowly, waiting for them to catch me up! Certainly, my badgers were a lot better off than any other young badgers that year as the summer was exceptionally hot and it must have made digging for earthworms almost impossible.

It is at this time of year that many complaints are voiced by gardeners about the damage that badgers do in their garden. When people ring me up and complain they have a badger in their garden, I try to remark 'Aren't you lucky' before they have a chance to tell me any more because I know what is going to be said next. People who look after their gardens frequently water, weed and tend the ground, constantly turning it over, which keeps the soil loose and moist. Earthworms and beetles can live near the surface. So if you are a badger, in dry weather, a garden like this (or a golf course) can be most attractive. The fact that, in very severe cases, it can look as though a cultivator has been used, does not endear badgers to the owner. This is a problem which generally rectifies itself as soon as the weather changes, and in the short term, can be overcome by actually putting food out for the badgers. But the hardest part is to persuade the complainant to put food out for the 'dear little things' after all the damage they have done.

I was now walking the badgers every day, and always the same way. We would walk up the alleyways of the homeground, around to the old cider orchard and back through the sheep paddock. I was basically teaching them their permanent paths. Establishing a territory for them, we again had no problem with other badgers dunging on the paths that we used, to show that they objected to the cubs. Maybe, as we had walked them as youngsters who offered no threat, they had been accepted. By August the cubs were beginning to turn nocturnal and I could no longer walk them during daylight. They would only go at dusk or late at night. I took a torch with me so that I could check to see they were all with me, but often there was enough moonlight to see their striped heads and one soon gets accustomed to night light.

We had not had rain for many, many weeks. One night I was nearing the end of our walk, going through the sheep paddock. With two cubs close by me, I could see the other cub about ten yards away, but suddenly realized that there was another black and white head only fifteen yards to my left. Checking with my torch, I was amazed to see that we had been joined by another badger, probably from our neighbouring sett. I dared not show my excitement and carried on walking, and the stranger eventually moved off back to the hedgerow. I am sure that badgers have to extend their territories when food is scarce, and indeed I have had 'extra' badgers on two other occasions during the dry spell. Not only had they accepted the cubs but obviously felt that I was no threat either.

Each night, I would take their food down to the pen and leave it on the side, while we went for our walk. Charging out of their temporary sett as soon as they heard me, I would be greeted by the lovely sound that they make to each other. It is really like a soft purr sounding 'Uv vuv vuv vuv vuv', and immediately they would scent my feet. They would bound off together, and as they got older the more confident they became, running off and exploring, and meeting up with me as I went around the fields, although Bluebell, whom I had a special relationship with, remained with me most of the time. The individual personalities became more evident as they grew, with Willow ever the one to get into trouble. If anyone would go missing it was bound to be Willow, who would turn up in his own good time; but the evidence of his disappearance always showed itself the next day in daylight by the odd hole dug under gates, turned-over litter bins, and even a methodically emptied fridge in the feed store when the door was found to be easy to open. A crate of milk with the top taken off every single bottle and one and a half inches of milk drunk from each one was the work of his lordship, and I really think he would have gone a long way in a welly-throwing competition judging by the chaos he caused in the backhouse, where usually our boots are stored tidily in pairs along the wall! A basket of laundry, left by mistake on the floor by the washing machine, was an open invitation for fun as far as Willow was concerned, and clothing items were scattered for quite a distance. Knickers were still being found late the next morning – it was a good job the farm was not open at that time for visitors.

This was all very well, but if he did go missing, I would arrive back at the pen with both the girls and would have to shut them up, go back into the house for an hour and then go back down to the cowstall area and wait for the inevitable charge into the back of my legs that was Willow letting me know he had returned; I could then pen him as well and give them all their food. I could imagine both the girls, lying on their elbow and thinking, 'God, isn't he annoying!', having to wait for his return before they could have their food. I was never too happy either, but the underlying fear that he might not come home always guaranteed that I was pleased to see him no matter how long I had to wait.

When we did eventually get rain it came in abundance, and the first night it came the rain was really torrential. Right from when I was a child, I have always loved the rain, and the fact that I was already dripping from head to toe by the time I got down to the pen did not stop me looking forward to my nightly walk with the cubs. They were to share my feelings towards the rain and revelled in the streams of water running through the yard. Primrose found where the guttering along the cowstall was blocked causing it to overflow, the water cascading on to the floor below. Standing on her hind legs, she pointed her nose up to the supply of water and allowed the droplets to shower through her thick coat. Joining in with their excitement, I chased the cubs around; arching their backs, they would shake their heads and jump with all four feet in the air in a sideways movement. When they used to get excited like this they would very often make all their fur stand on end which made them look like huge fluff balls; this, I believe, is also something they do in moments of fear to make themselves look much, much larger. A good half an hour was spent chasing around before we even started our walk that evening. It was at times like those that I used to think it was just as well it was nearly the middle of the night, because if anyone could have seen me they would have thought I was completely mad. I would try and walk the badgers as near to midnight as possible. This was so that, if any of them went missing, at least I knew there would be less traffic around should they stray towards the roads.

On occasions, but not very often, Derek would come with me (more out of a sense of duty than pleasure) and walk the alleyways with us, but his lack of keenness was more due to the pain inflicted during the walk rather than to any dislike of badgers. When walking the badgers, particularly in the old cider orchard where the grass was long, we were included in their games, and to avoid the playful charges which ended with a sharp nip was quite an art. Derek unfortunately never grasped this skill, and it was a good thing that no one could hear us out there at night as his vocal reactions to being 'caught' were often as colourful as his bruises.

My nightly walks gave me time on my own, and I often thought how lucky I was that Derek accepted the amount of time that my wildlife work takes up. The complete change from dairy farm to tourist attraction could never have been that easy, and although as a farmer he cared deeply for his animals he would never have the patience to care for small things that are orphaned or injured. He now has to put up with collecting all sorts of animals, holding orphans between feeds and even having fox cubs chewing his slippered feet whilst he tries to read his paper. I will not go as far as to say that all this is done without *any* complaints whatsoever, but as a husband he is very understanding, and my best friend too.

It is not until you have a reason to walk at night on a regular basis that you become aware of the creatures you share the night with. I had the pleasure on many occasions to see a barn owl gliding along the hedgerow, completely silent in its flight. The calling of the little owl was a nightly occurrence and he would change his roost from tree to tree as we walked the fields. The 'plop' of the water voles could be heard as we skirted the rhines, into the old cider orchard where a sparrowhawk could always be seen on his nightly perch on the same tree. Very often the fox would be weaving his way across the top of the homeground, never showing any great fear of us as he would just change his course and move away from us. It was an insight into badger behaviour too, to watch their play and foraging. I wonder if wild badgers tease like ours did. The three would very often go up to the Hereford bull who had already lain down and warmed his patch of grass for the night. They would go forward and sniff him, moving back and going forward again, making him move his majestic head to try and make out what they were doing. When the bull had decided it was necessary to rise up and find out exactly what they were up to, the badgers would lose interest immediately and move off as if their sole intention had been to make him get up – 'now let's go and find something else to do!' Their speed was also something that surprised me; one evening Willow disappeared into the discarded plastic cover from the silage, to emerge triumphantly with a screaming mole which quickly died from the shock.

The one thought that was constantly on my mind was how exactly we were going to release the cubs. Simon King contacted us and did a small amount of filming with the cubs, and I chatted with him over the problem. Eunice Overend was another person who very kindly offered much advice and, between the three of us, we designed the observation sett. I sweet-talked Derek into letting me have four sections of his silage pit, which was no longer used, and this would give me a 40-foot enclosure which was concrete-based. Taking some tunnels from the side of the enclosure through into what was a long feeder, we could create a high-sided alleyway which then took them into an old cowshed building where the chambers could be built. The next problem was finance. The local press had taken pictures of me walking the badgers and there was a lot of local interest in them, so we started an appeal to build them a home. A bus company called 'Badgerline' offered, for obvious reasons, to help and they gave sponsorship both to the building of the sett and also to the interpretations material displayed inside the building for visitors to learn more about badgers in general. Many people donated to the appeal, but without the help of Badgerline the sett would not have been possible. Luckily, a personal friend, Roger Gullidge, was a builder and he gave his own time free of charge; local firms supplied building materials either donated free of charge or at cost price so that a new home for Willow, Bluebell and Primrose became possible. The cement firm ARC even donated some ready-mix concrete so that the badgers could have a pond large enough to swim in built in the enclosure; the sight of Bluebell covered in duckweed during the summer is proof of its constant use.

From the chambers to the alleyways and out into the enclosure, it all faced the same way as the badgers were used to walking, and the special 'badger gate' opened out into the homeground where we walked. Badger gates consist of a piece of heavy timber suspended from a wooden frame. They are often put into fences erected by forestry companies trying to protect young plantations from dear and rabbits. They recognize that the badger is a friend to them, often killing rabbits, voles and mice. Fencing put along a territorial path would merely be uprooted or dug under by resident badgers to continue their access to their foraging area; this, in turn, would then also allow access to the rabbit. But a heavy gate which swings freely both ways can be pushed open by an animal as powerful as a badger, but something like a rabbit would not be strong enough; this way the badger still has access and the fence remains effective.

Building work commenced, and as the chambers and tunnels started to take shape, the evening walks were preceded by Willow, Primrose and Bluebell exploring the layout of what was to be their new home. Elated, they would climb up and down the tunnels, snorting in fun as they came unexpectedly face to face with each other.

The only thing that overshadowed this time for me, was fear for the safety of the badgers. I had by now become a member of the Somerset Trust Badger Group and was learning more and more about badgers, but also of the numbers of animals, estimated at 10,000 each year, that are taken for badger digging or baiting. This sport, if you can call it such a thing, involves using terriers to trap the badger underground so that men can dig down and extract the animals; these are either shot dead straight away, or worse still, pitted against larger dogs actually on the location. Other times they are transported to secret destinations where the fight can be watched and bets can be laid. As the badger is such a powerful animal, often the jaw or legs would be broken to put the badger at a disadvantage before the dogs are put with them, but even then a 'good fight' can sometimes last three hours, inflicting horrendous wounds on the dog and the final release from terror for the badger as it dies.

My fear, with all the publicity that we had received, was for the safety of my three with the location of their home being general knowledge. Many a night I would wake up and lie there, straining to hear any noise that was unusual. This is still something that I worry about. Fortunately, a local firm from Yeovil called Guest Security has installed an alarm system free of charge to protect the badgers on the farm. The badger seems close to the heart of many people.

It was now November and the big day arrived: the sett was completed and it was time to move the cubs in. The only thing we were slightly worried about was getting them used to the soft lights in the chambers. We turned the lights on full so that the cubs could see all around, and decided to return after a while to turn the lights down if they had settled. Derek came with us as we took our usual walk, and on returning, I put the food in the alleyways and shut the gate. After watching them for a short time, we returned to the house for a cup of coffee. Half an hour later we crept back to see if all was well, to be met with the sight of three badgers curled up together in one of the chambers, fast asleep, contented and very much at home.

I continued to walk them until the beginning of January 1990. By then we would all start together, then they would go their own way and the rest of the walk was punctuated by a badger chasing up to say hello and then dashing off into the night. My torch would pick them up foraging in the fields, or as I went back to the house I would meet them wandering through the gardens and around the outhouses.

From then, I decided to leave the badger gate open all the time so that they could come and go as they pleased. I hoped they would stay and maybe have cubs of their own, one day. This was their territory now, an area they had come to know so well and a home they had readily accepted just as I had when, in 1977, I first came to the farm.

5

Owls: Sage Makes his Mark

It was a lovely sunny, summer's evening that found us on our way to the local school to attend a lecture on owls by Mr David Chaffe. Our youngest boys, then aged 9 and 10 years, were keen to go and Derek had always had an interest in birds (the feathered variety!) so the outstanding chores were forgotten about, and we all went along.

We are lucky to have a thriving village school at each end of our road. They hold many events through the year which always attract the local villagers and give everyone a chance to meet up and socialize. This was West Huntspill School that we were going to, with its large playground and attractive grassed areas. We entered the school by the door where the old school bell still hangs, and passed the colourful displays of all the children's work covering the corridor walls. In the classrooms tiny chairs and tables were stacked ready for the morning cleaners. The talk was to be held in the hall which was crowded with parents and children, and the usual gabble was heard as we chatted whilst waiting for the evening to start. The Headmaster introduced David Chaffe who went on to hold the audience spellbound as he described the birds of our countryside. Demanding total silence, he brought in birds to show us; such was the interest that not a sound was uttered. It was the first time that I had really had the chance to see owls and hawks at such close proximity, and whilst it is always better to see such birds free, there must also be a place for education like this – so that people can see the beauty of such birds and appreciate the importance of maintaining the balance of our environment, to guarantee the sight of such creatures in our countryside.

First we saw the kestrel, a bird that hovers with its tail feathers spread in a fan as it pinpoints its prey, which is caught as the bird dives to the ground. Many are now seen on the sides of the motorway as they make the most of the food supply of field voles, thriving in the rough grass of the 'no man's land' that borders the fast lanes. Although fairly similar in their colouring, they are not to be confused with the sparrowhawk, whose flight pattern is entirely different, swooping over hedgerows, catching small birds completely by surprise.

The little owl charmed everyone. No taller than a bag of sugar, it sat bobbing up and down, just as interested in seeing us as we in him. The bright orange iris of his eyes gave him such an angry look which was certainly not helped by the wispy eyebrows – a miniature Denis Healey! He was standing stoutly on his little yellow legs. His brown chest, which was speckled with white, was puffed out and he made it quite evident that what he lacked in size, he made up for in character.

Next was the tawny owl, which was three times the size of the little owl. Shades of dappled chestnut brown were accentuated by the evening sun streaming through the windows. Slowly blinking each eye independently, as she swivelled her head to take in her surroundings, she had an almost regal composure – such a beautiful bird, whose mellow hooting is heard in towns as well as the countryside.

People often think that you need to go abroad to see colourful birds, but when the barn owl was brought in, it was quite evident that we also have birds whose colouring has to be seen to be believed. Often barn owls are thought to be pure white as they are usually seen in flight. The complete underneath of the barn owl is white and this, together with special feathers that give silent flight, would lead an unsuspecting field vole to take it as clouds drifting by – until the strong talons pounce with such force that the animal is killed on impact. It must be those big eyes that attract so many people to owls, when in fact they are very efficient killers. The body of the barn owl is shaded with different hues of honey brown, bejewelled with grey speckling which affords such good camouflage that, when they pull their wings around them and close their eyes, when roosted by hay or straw in barns, they merge into the background. A frill of white feathers frames the heart-shaped face, which is in fact another part of its hunting equipment: the heart-shape forms two funnels carrying sound to the ears, which are on different levels to help pinpoint sound. The barn owl is the only owl that can hunt by sound alone.

We were to hear that the numbers of barn owls had reduced dramatically since the Second World War, due mainly to strong pesticides causing devastation in the food chain, and that release schemes were being organized to try to increase the population. We had already been open to the public for a year and there were several places on the farm where an aviary could be built, so we stayed behind after the talk to discuss with David the possibility of having a pair for breeding. We returned home, excited at the thought of having some barn owls. Derek had not seen one on the farm for years and, being so close to the Somerset Levels, the habitat should be right for them.

A few months went by: the aviary was built and the boxes installed. Placed in a quiet corner of the yard, the aviary was screened by some conifers, giving the birds the seclusion that they prefer. David supplied us with a pair. The female was captive-bred. The male had an injured wing and could never return to the wild; having adapted to life in captivity, it had paired with the female and they were duly installed. We had little contact with them, only going into the aviary to put the food in, as it was important for them to retain their wildness. In February the following year our first egg was laid, and the female went on to lay a brood of five eggs at two-day intervals. She incubated the eggs from the time that the first egg was laid, so they hatched out at different times. This meant that eventually there were five ugly-looking chicks, that looked more like vultures, in various sizes. There are times during their growth when a chick will eat twice as much as an adult, so in the wild, if food becomes scarce, the big chick will eat the little chick to ensure survival; in captivity, the food supply is controlled and they can all get plenty to eat.

Weeks went by, and at the age of two months their appearance had improved thank goodness! We now had five different sized balls of fluff with their heart-shaped faces becoming very evident. Although not old enough to stand up on their legs, they would squat on their hocks and show off their ability to turn their heads upside down. Bobbing and moving their heads in circles, they would thrust their faces forward to focus their eyes in the most comical positions – they were great time-wasters!

At three months they had their adult plumage and it was becoming increasingly difficult to tell them apart from their parents. They were then moved into an adjoining aviary which had an escape hatch. Two months later, when they had got used to their new pen, the hatch was opened and they were given their freedom, although we continued to leave food in the aviary until we were sure they were catching their own food. What usually happens is that, after release, we continue to leave dead chicks in the aviary, which they return for, but once they come in and just eat the heads of the chicks (which is presumed a delicacy) you know they are catching enough not to bother with eating the whole chick.

We had a shed near the aviary where I used to set broody hens with eggs. The shed was fox-proof, but I had not thought of the gaps in the roof as an access. On one of my evening patrols, I checked the broodies and was pleased to find that one hen had hatched out five peacock chicks. They are very pretty chicks, their fluff being almost like velvet, and they have a very plaintive cry. I made a mental note that she would need to go into a run with them the next morning, but I am sure you have guessed what happened. By the next morning all that remained was five headless bodies scattered near the sitting hen, where they had strayed from their mother early in the morning to peck around – probably not all that far, but their plaintive cries would have attracted the young owls who were still returning for food. The only difference the owls would have noticed from the usual food left available to them was that dinner was warm today. Nature does not always say thank you.

The next year we released three, and by the following year we had reports of a pair being established on the south side of us, and another pair living by the river. In fact, this pair was seen the next year with five young. From then on, all our young captive-reared owls were passed on to the RSPCA's Wildlife Unit near Taunton for release as we felt that the pairs either side of us were now populating without any help from us. We still see barn owls flying through the yard now, several years on, so we hope they are descendants of the ones that we released originally.

The birds sent down to the RSPCA are released by special people who are licensed to do so and who monitor the birds after release, and indeed can tell us if the birds have successfully bred. The birds can be taken as a group while they are still too young to fly. They are housed in an owl box, in a suitable position, and are fed there, so that by the time they take their first flight, they have become used to their surroundings and hopefully they stay. If the owls to be released are older birds, unrelated pairs are put in a barn where they are contained. Once they breed and are still feeding their young, freedom is then given to them. The parents then naturally return to the roost in order to rear their family.

All owls released have rings put on them, and this can help monitor the success of the programme. If you find a dead or injured bird, it is important to notify the Department of the Environment with the number; they can then trace the owner, and help with their records. Even some badgers that are released are tattooed for the same reason. I was told a lovely story by a badger fan, who was himself a policeman, until due to an accident he had to retire and took on a traffic control job. Knowing that police often see badgers on the side of the road, whenever possible he would get officers to give him the location of any sightings, and also encourage them to check whether the animal was in fact dead and if it was carrying a tattoo. These details he would log, and it helped with pinpointing blackspots on roads involving badgers. You can imagine he became quite well known for this in a good-humoured way, and most patrolmen would go along with it.

It was halfway through the night that the message came through to him: a colleague had passed a badger and was going back to investigate.

'Traffic Control, Traffic Control, I confirm dead badger on left-hand side of A429 approximately 100 yards from the "Flying Duck" Public House', said the patrolman.

'431, 431, I am receiving you. Did you see if there was a tattoo on the animal?' replied the 'badger fanatic'.

Feeling this was taking things a bit too far, the patrolman said: 'Traffic Control, Traffic Control, I must admit, I never thought to look for that!'

Trying to be as persuasive as ever, the 'badger fanatic' said: '431, 431, I would most appreciate it if you could just check for me, mate.'

Following a sigh, the line went dead as it was supposed the officer had gone back to see. Several minutes later he returned:

'Traffic Control, Traffic Control, I have checked the animal', said the patrolman.

'431, 431, thank you so much, did the animal have a tattoo?' asked the 'badger fanatic'.

'Traffic Control, Traffic Control, yes it did' was the reply.

'Oh, good! 431, 431, what did it say and what part of the animal was it on?'

'Traffic Control, Traffic Control, the tattoo was on the left back leg.'

'Yes?'

'It was a heart with an arrow going through it, saying I love Lucy!'

I think the poor man is still getting his leg pulled over this even now.

It was through one of our visitors coming to the farm that Sage came to us. Sage is a barn owl, who was hand-reared by a young lad called Peter, who hatched the egg in an incubator. The egg came from a captive female who rejected the brood, and it successfully hatched. Sage is completely imprinted, which is what happens when a bird or an animal is reared on its own. The only thing it sees is you, and it will grow up thinking it is a human being and unable to relate to its own species. This means that it will never be able to be released as the creature would be unable to fend for itself. Peter was very good with him, and although he kept him in a flat, he would often take him out to the countryside in the car to fly him for exercise. Sage was so tame that he would travel on the back of the passenger seat as good as gold. Brought up in a house, he was at home anywhere and used to people and traffic.

However, due to pressure of work, Peter was finding that he could not give Sage as much time as he wanted. It was Peter's father who visited us one day; seeing the way we kept our animals, he suggested to Peter that he came to see us, which he did, and after much discussion Sage came to us. Peter still visits him occasionally and takes him out – seven years later Sage still knows his whistle. I am sure we underestimate the memory that animals and birds do have. Although he has an aviary of his own, there is nothing that Sage would rather do than to come out and meet people. He is super for educational talks and shows. Many a person following our car has been surprised to realize that it is a real owl sitting on the back of the seat enjoying the ride! The only problem with his being mixed up is that, although he is very good with people, he would attack another bird or animal if one came near. Being a very affectionate bird he will often demonstrate his affection by mating on your shoulder, which can not only prove embarrassing when people ask you 'What's he doing?' but also means that you end up with white stains down your back! He now shares an aviary with our herd of tortoises, as even his talons cannot pierce their shells. It is a good compromise, with the tortoises having the pen for exercise during the day and Sage having it as a flight at night!

We took him to the Food and Farming Show at Hyde Park in London in 1989, and because it was a three-day event, we kept him in a horse trailer at night with a piece of wire over the back to make it secure. Unbeknown to us, on the second day, someone moved the trailer to allow a car to get out and failed to replace the wire properly. Busy getting ready for the coming day, I walked round to the trailer to get Sage out. Carefully opening the side door, I glanced inside, but was not unduly worried when at first I could not see him. He is a great one for getting into a corner and I thought the branch that was placed in the trailer for him to perch on was probably hiding him. As I looked further the truth began to dawn, and on seeing the loose netting, my worst fear was realized. Climbing out, I leant with my back to the trailer. With my stomach churning, I looked towards the security fences and I could see the morning traffic building up, buses, taxis, cars speeding down the lanes. God, where could he be? He would never be able to find his own food, or could so easily be picked up by someone who had no idea of how to look after him. Guilt flooded in. I should have checked and double-checked the wire, I should never have brought him here. With tears stinging my eyes, I went to find Clive and Simon, who were with me. We reported it to the security people in case they had any news, and the details were soon flashed across the showground by walkie-talkies. We wandered looking for him, but there were so many places he could hide even if he had stayed in the area. I would not want to go through those two hours again. Hopes were raised when a security officer said that he had seen a large bird on the top of the tent at about 2.30 a.m., but it had flown down towards the Serpentine. He was good as lost. Trying to continue with the show, it was hard to concentrate on what we were meant to be doing.

Exactly two hours and twenty minutes after we realized that he was missing, he was returned to us. He had been handed in to the falconry stand at the show. Sage had slipped out of the trailer and flown from the tent down towards the river, landing in one of the large trees by the security fences. As he made himself comfortable on a branch, some tawny owls were upset at having to share their tree and started to hoot their disapproval. It was now nearly four in the morning and two young police officers were patrolling the fences; being bored silly, they decided to hoot back up into the trees to these owls. Sage thought they were calling him, and a very startled police constable found himself with a very amiable barn owl sitting on his shoulder. I believe it took quite some time for him to convince his superior officer, when contacting him by radio, as to his predicament. Having been taken safely into custody Sage was duly sent to the Hawk Centre on the showground and eventually passed back to us.

An exciting break for him maybe, what with meeting the Duke of Edinburgh and the great escape, but not something that I would want to experience again!

We are very careful, when we take Sage out, to make people realize that barn owls should not be kept as pets. They are beautiful birds, but we must get their habitat right so that we can see them in the wild where they belong. Because our homeground is divided into paddocks for people to walk round, it naturally leaves areas of long grass extending from the hedgerow and thus increasing the hunting ground that they need. Chris Sperring, who has been involved with barn owls for some time, has been encouraging farmers in Avon to leave this corridor of long grass around their fields and it has been successful in increasing the numbers of barn owls in residence. It is estimated that there are only 9,000 barn owls in the wild, and yet there are between 20,000 and 30,000 in captivity. Release schemes have not proved successful unless carried out correctly. Thousands of birds were being released from captive pairs, not taking into account the habitat they were going into, and these were basically doomed to die. Now new licences are being introduced to control the numbers in captivity and also breeding for release. Barn owls must only be released in areas where the habitat is suitable and the territory is not already being used by a resident pair. Much research must be done before the birds are finally let go – it is not just a question of opening a hatch and away they go. It is a worry that many of our barns and old buildings are being modernized and used as houses, but I do not think it is a question of losing nesting sites as much as the loss of food supply. Farming methods have changed. At one time hay was the main source of winter food for the farm animals, and the hay would be stored in every conceivable outhouse or barn to be kept dry for the winter. The seeds would attract mice and rats, and if the winter became severe, the barn owls could go where there was a store of hay and be sure of a few meals before the milder weather came. Now we make silage, a much better feed, but one that is wrapped in black polythene bags to ferment until opened for feeding. It is important for the fermentation that no air is allowed into the bags, and the last thing you want is rats and mice nibbling at them. So as the rows are stored, bait is laid between the round bales to control the vermin, which it does quite successfully; but this is no help to the barn owl.

. . . very amiable barn owl sitting on his shoulder.

Sage very often, especially in the winter, comes into the house. When we lived downstairs, his favourite perch was on top of the bureau/bookcase. We had the bank manager coming to see us one afternoon (as we do each year to see if he will lend us more money to get through the winter!) and I had forgotten Sage was in the room. Mr Curtice arrived, and was reverently shown to the front room and offered a cup of tea to get us off on the right foot. I suddenly realized, as Sage flew a quick circuit of the room, that he was still around. Laughing, the bank manager said it was all right, and that we should leave Sage in the room. Draping his coat over the dining-room chair, Mr Curtice made himself comfortable by the fire and heard all our explanations as to why there was not so much money in the bank as there should be. Apart from a couple more circuits, Sage behaved very well and did not disturb the proceedings. Once all had been discussed and we had reached agreement, Mr Curtice rose to leave. Commenting on what a beautiful bird Sage was, he shook our hands. Helping him on with his coat we thanked him for being so understanding. He turned to leave and, as I followed to show him out, I noticed, to my horror, a large white stain that ran from the collar down almost to the hem, right down the middle of the back of his coat. When Sage had done one of his quick circuits, he had obviously dropped a package that no one had noticed. At the door Mr Curtice turned and smiled, thanking me for an entertaining afternoon. I just could not think of what to say and found myself just saying goodbye and shutting the door quietly behind him. Surely he would not give us the extra overdraft after that!

Mr Curtice was a very popular person, with a keen sense of humour. The next day a letter arrived detailing what we had talked about, and concluding with the remark that: 'I trust that I have covered all the points that we discussed (the owl, I'm sure, will confirm this, after making his presence known!) and I look forward to seeing you both soon. Kind regards, Tony Curtice.'

Many owls come to us either as orphans or, more usually, from road traffic accidents. Birds of prey often hunt near the motorways on the grass verges, and being so light they can often get caught in the slipstream of vehicles, with nasty results. Young birds of prey, found sometimes when trees are felled, or when they themselves have fallen out of trees, are easier to deal with than smaller birds when taken into care, as they usually can withstand the trauma of being picked up and handled. However, even at quite an early age, they are capable of using their talons to object to your intrusion, so they must be treated with respect. Because birds of prey eat their food whole, they regurgitate a pellet each day which contains all the fur, feather and bones that they have swallowed, and the rest is digested in the usual way. So it is necessary, while these birds are being held captive, to feed them on whole food to keep this form of digestion going. We buy in dead chicks from local hatcheries and freeze them, fifteen to a bag, to use as food. The male chicks are killed at one day old because, being a light breed, they will never fatten and so are not commercially viable. Zoos and reptile keepers also use chicks as feed. It took quite some time before I could get used to feeding them to the animals. It was not so bad with the large owls as they eat them whole, but small owls and youngsters need their food cut up; but I have progressed from saying sorry, looking away and using a meat cleaver to halve them, to actually cutting them up with a knife. You have to be prepared to do all sorts when involved with wildlife – they don't have knives and forks out there!

I found it fascinating, when given some barn owl eggs to incubate, that when hatched, the chicks required meat straight away, even though it was pieces just the size of the head of a match. The little chicks' bodies were only the size of the old tenpenny piece, so you can imagine just how tiny their meat needed to be. Still slightly squeamish when cutting up dead chicks, I had this marvellous idea that maybe they could be done in a processor! I tell you now, for those impressed with this thinking, that it is not such a good idea as the legs and eyes do not process – the sight of them flailing around the bowl makes one decide that next time you will use a knife!

I love little owls as they are such fierce-looking characters, but there was one who had me looking for him for ages. We have a special sick room in a quiet area with several wardrobes converted into owl cages. Shelves hold more cages, infra-red lamps are suspended over surfaces for casualties requiring heat, cupboards hold the medicines and equipment and drawers hold all the clean fresh blankets to go in the cages. This little owl was underweight when he came in, but had picked up well and would soon be ready for release. I opened his cage and disinfected the floor; as usual he sat on the shelf bobbing his disgust at my intrusion. I turned and took a fresh towel from the drawer, shut it and carried on with cleaning the cage, only to realize halfway through that he was no longer sitting on the shelf. The first place to look was on top of all the cages, although I certainly had not heard him fly. I pulled all the cages out to see if he had gone behind. Next, all the reference books had to come off the shelf in case he was behind there, and by this time I was beginning to think I was going silly. There were not that many places he could hide. Pulling out the medicine cupboard. I could see I had drawn a blank there; and unless he was a highly qualified limbo dancer, there was no way that he could have got under the door. My last resort, as you have probably guessed, was to look in the drawer, and immediately a little brown face with those wispy eyebrows popped up from the corner of the drawer. He must have been so quick to have dived in there in the short time it took to pull out the towel and shut the drawer again. That wasted at least three-quarters of an hour: lessons numbers one and two when dealing with wildlife – patience and a sense of humour.

Maybe the prettiest owlet is the tawny; many are found having fallen out of the nest and usually, when left alone, they can climb back up the tree and into the nest. The only problem is that someone else could find them and may not be so knowledgeable as to what to do with them, so it is probably best to pick them up and take them to a rescue centre. We had one recently who was a real character and who spent most of his time looking down from the care room window at the visitors below. He, like all our other bird orphans, went on down to the RSPCA's Wildlife Centre to be assessed and kept in a large aviary to exercise before being released. We do not have the correct pens away from the public eye to keep them right up to the point of release, and we were sorry to see him go. After having them confined in a care pen, it is only when birds are placed in a larger aviary that you can assess how well they can fly and how fit they are; often they will relax and show signs of injury when they feel they are not being watched. So the pens at the wildlife unit are designed so that the inmates can be observed whilst unaware of people being around. To release too soon can undo all the good work that has been put into the creature's convalescence.

Jo was a beautiful tawny owl, who came to us from a friend called Cheri Vincent. She had two tawny owls in separate aviaries that she had cared for, Jo, and another called Hoot who was blind in one eye. Every year Hoot would lay eggs and try to brood them. She would sit on them for so long, but without a male to fertilize the eggs they never hatched, and Cheri really felt sorry for her. But one year, chance brought a very young tawny owlet to Cheri just as Hoot was sitting, and with great trepidation, Cheri tried Hoot with the owlet: she took to her immediately. She fed and protected her – so much so that Cheri had to be careful when she went into the aviary in case Hoot misread her actions. Once fully fledged, the young tawny was ready to go, and being completely healthy she should survive; but this posed a problem to Cheri as she could not release the mother. Cheri offered Jo to us in order to gain more space so that she could split Hoot and her 'offspring' with the eventual aim of releasing the youngster from the adjoining pen. She hoped that the tie with her mother would bring her back to feed, until such a time as she was capable of looking after herself. This was in fact what happened.

When Jo arrived we put her in an aviary by the barn owls. We very rarely see tawny owls on our farm although there are some living further down our road. It was a lovely sound, to hear the hooting in the evening, but after a couple of nights, I realized as I went out to feed the badgers that there were two owls calling. Standing quietly in the yard, I eventually pinpointed the noise. Another tawny was sitting on top of our telephone wire pole, hooting to Jo, who was returning the call. Talking to Derek about it, we wondered if it was a male tawny who was attracted to Jo or one that was objecting to a strange owl being on their territory. All winter, without fail, every evening the owl would come to the pole and call to Jo. It is at times like these that it is not easy to make decisions. If it was a mate, were we cruel to keep Jo penned up without a chance of ever pairing and mating? There again, would she be able to survive and catch her own food? Finding food was not really a problem, as Jo was used to her aviary and surroundings after being there for more than six months, and would be capable of returning for food. We were also scattering food around the various setts that our young badgers had built around the farm, so this was another food source: so we made the decision to let her go. They have not been seen or heard of since on the farm. Maybe he whisked her away to his territory to build a new home. We certainly miss the lovely sound of them calling to each other.

One casualty that came here travelled a very long way. A friend of mine, Kate, was doing research work on Skomer Island, and they found a young short-eared owl that had been attacked by the seagulls. Usually, everyone accepts that there are always fatalities in the wild and leaves well alone, but this little chap seemed to be a fighter and they asked if they could take him ashore and get some veterinary advice. Amazingly, he survived the journey to Somerset and Kate kept him overnight at home. Bringing him over to me the next morning, he ate some food, which is always a good sign, and we left him to get over his ordeal. The next day he was taken to the vet, who diagnosed one of his legs as being broken and one wing as slightly damaged. Barry was prepared to operate the next day, but seeing as they had no dead chicks in stock to feed him, I took him home to return the next day for surgery. Unfortunately he died during the night. Possibly the ordeal of transporting, captivity and stress had taken its toll, but he would have certainly died anyway had he been left on the cliffside at Skomer. At least there had been the chance that he would survive with everyone's efforts, but it was not to be. It is at times like these that you will always feel disheartened, but as long as you can feel that you have done your best, you can do no more.

A few days later, one of our terrapins looked unwell so we made an appointment for Barry to see him. I was rather tied up in the office so Derek offered to take the terrapin in. Placing it in the box, I explained what symptoms the terrapin had; then suddenly remembering that the vet had no dead chicks in stock, I asked Derek to take a bag in with him for the vet to put in the freezer in case the surgery needed them at any time. When Derek returned, he explained that the terrapin was going to need a course of injections and Barry had decided to keep him in under observation. Four days later, we had a call to say that the terrapin was better and that we could pick him up. On arrival I found that all the vets were out, but Becky, the nurse, brought the terrapin out explaining that he no longer needed any treatment and was feeding well. She had put his defrosted dead chick for today in the box with him for us to feed him when we got home! Somewhere between here and the vet's the message had got mixed up, and the chicks that I had sent in to stock their freezer were taken as the food supply for the terrapin, and he had chomped his way through them quite happily. We had never thought to feed him on dead chicks before. Some things you can learn by mistake!

6

Derek's Friends: Foxes in the Toy Cupboard

The fox is one animal that is deemed to be a nuisance, yet surely it has as much right in the countryside as any other. It is actually capable, like all carnivores, of controlling its own population, and where it is hunted or where there is a plentiful food supply, it will breed more readily and in larger numbers. When left to its own devices, the main control of the animal's population is determined by its territory and availability of food. Indeed, many cases where foxes are blamed for attacks on poultry, if looked into, will show some lack of good husbandry. You would expect a fox to help himself if a poultry door has been forgotten and not shut up, and, at times, the rabbit hutches or poultry houses are not as substantial as they should be. Of course, there are exceptions, and after all the fox is a hunter.

The one problem that affects us more than anything is fox cubs. The fox is becoming more and more an urban animal, and can forage in dustbins and waste areas and find plenty of food that we humans throw out. They no longer have any real fear of people, and will make a den and cub quite close to places of human occupation. The cubs usually number between four and five, and as they are born on to bare earth, they are a dark chocolate colour which acts as camouflage. At three to four weeks the cubs will sometimes emerge from the den to play, although the vixen is not usually far away. This is the time when so many are picked up by people thinking they are lost, and sometimes not even knowing what they are.

Sometimes qualified people can make mistakes! Two cubs were found by some boys on waste land in the nearby town of Weston-super-Mare. They took them to a local vet who thought they were young puppies. He had a client whose labrador had unfortunately just lost her puppies, and he wondered if she would foster these 'pups'. He contacted the people concerned who were more than willing to try, and the puppies were duly dispatched to the labrador's home. She took to them straight away, cleaning and nuzzling them. They thought there were going to be no problems. Really there weren't. The 'pups' thrived and grew bigger every day, but it suddenly started to become very apparent what kind of 'pups' they were as they began to turn red and to develop pointed ears and noses. The scent glands were developing too, producing that unforgettable whiff. The difficulty was that here were two fox cubs brought up in totally domestic surroundings, who absolutely adored people and dogs. It would seem totally impossible to be able to release them back into the wild.

Knowing of us, they asked if we would take them; we agreed to do so, saying that we would keep them with our foxes but should they revert to being wild, they would go to the RSPCA for release. When they arrived, Willow was in the house at night on his own and so they shared the airing cupboard with him for a few days. We took the fox cubs up with us when we went to the Food and Farming Exhibition in London; how wonderful that Fate had given us the chance to take these animals with us as well, fox cubs that were completely used to people and noise. The sight of fox cubs squabbling and playing tag was really enchanting as they are so pretty at that age. On our return they moved into the fox pen with our older ones and related to them straight away, with more freedom and no more contact with those involved in rearing them. In two weeks they had reverted to being wild and, I am pleased to say, went to the RSPCA for release. There the fox cubs are put into large compounds with food just thrown in to them to make sure that the wild instinct has returned. They fight and squabble over their food and have a pecking order within the group, much as it would be in the wild. The foxes are eventually released, healthy and vaccinated, into release sites where foxes are condoned and which are hunt-free. This is from the age of six months when dispersal from the family group would occur anyway.

One day we received a call from a lady who was worried that she had three fox cubs in her garden all on their own. She wanted to know what to do. Talking details through with her we came to the conclusion that a vixen had made a home under the shed in the lady's garden and the cubs were merely coming out for some exercise. Left alone, as they were not stressed in any way, they would return to the den to be looked after by the mother. In all probability, they would be reared and would finally disperse without causing any trouble, and she might never see them again. The lady was quite happy with this, and rang again three months later to say that she and her family had had the pleasure of watching the foxes grow; it had now been some time since they had seen the vixen and her cubs and they assumed that the 'fox family' had finally gone.

If you see fox cubs, please do not pick them up. Stand and watch from a distance: the vixen is usually not far away, and left to their own devices the cubs know their own way home. Only pick them up if they are distressed and obviously in need of care. In 1992 the RSPCA Wildlife Unit had to cope with over ninety fox cubs. That is a lot of release sites to be found, and no one, no matter how hard we try, will be able to teach these fox cubs the way to survive in the wild better than their mother.

Our first encounter with foxes was when Gordon and Bennet came to us from Chertsey, near London. They were two male foxes offered to us if we could give them a good home. Their names were derived from the husband's feeling on the matter when his wife brought them home after finding them when out walking the dog. Gordon and Bennet were now six months old and only had limited accommodation. Totally imprinted, they were used to their food being served up twice a day and were very friendly. It was highly unlikely that they would ever be suitable for release. Having built a new pen for them, I went and collected them. It was really the first chance I had had to study a fox properly. Each fox was quite different. Bennet had black legs and the guard hairs on his coat were black as well, giving him a much darker appearance than Gordon who was a lovely honey colour; both had the white/grey throat and white tip to their tails – or should I say brush? Their eyes were bright orange and had a slit in the centre like a cat's eye, no doubt adapting at night to give better

Fox cub Heidi, at just one week old

Heidi hiding in the grass

Heidi enjoys a snooze in the toy cupboard

Two sly looking characters – Gordon and Bennett

A handful of pin cushions

Feeding time, at 2-3 weeks old

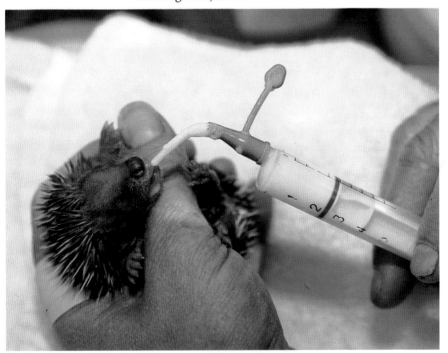

Young dormouse, one of a rescued family nursed back to health

Murphy the mink, just a baby

Armful of trouble

Bramble, the little roedeer, at 3 weeks old

Bramble enjoying a bottle – he measured just 15 inches from the tip of his ears to his toes

Anyone up the chimney? Bluebell investigates

Still just a baby – Bluebell with her Mum

vision as they are mainly nocturnal animals, though they can be seen sometimes during the day.

Their first night was spent cowering in the house in the corner of the pen, but the next day showed a much braver pair more inquisitive about their new pen and definitely friendly. As they rolled on their backs to have their tummies tickled, I could feel the very dense soft fur, rather like a rabbit's fur. In the wild they spend little time underground, usually lying up under hedges or even in trees. With a coat as thick as that they would be plenty warm enough. I was amazed how agile they were, jumping up on the rafters of the pen, which were only four inches wide, and running confidently around the wire. In a way they are very cat-like; this is because their diet consists largely of voles and mice and they require the same abilities as cats to catch their prey. Foxes do a 'mouse leap'. They have very acute hearing; standing still, they will listen to the sound of the rustle to locate where their rodent victim is. Then leaping up, high above the intended victim, they steer themselves with their tail, landing with full force and placing their front feet on their quarry, making escape impossible.

Gordon was slightly friendlier than Bennet and we often took him for a walk on a lead, but it was not easy: unlike a dog, a fox prefers to go along (or through!) hedges and will never walk in a straight line. One thing I did notice with them was that they were very wary when the badgers were roaming around and would go along the side of their pen. I think foxes respect the power of a badger. They are sometimes found living alongside, but are not such a clean animal as the badger. They leave remnants of prey outside of the home, food that has been brought back to be eaten. Discarded feathers and parts of corpses at the entrance of a hole is definite evidence that a fox is in residence. It has sometimes been thought that you could cross a fox with a dog, but they are a completely different species and their bodies do not contain the same number of chromosomes so it is therefore impossible. Sadly, we no longer have Bennet but Gordon, at the ripe age of eight years at the time of writing, is still with us and acts as 'foster dad' in the interim period that we sometimes house fox cubs prior to release. On the occasions when cubs have mistaken him for a vixen and latched on to him in the hopes of some milk, he has in no uncertain terms made the situation quite clear!

Derek, with his farmer instincts, has never been too keen on foxes, and there was one fox that we both objected to. It was the second year after we had opened to the public, when we had over a hundred free-range hens in the orchard. Visitors were amazed to see a fox come through the homeground into the orchard, calmly collecting a chicken and walking back home. This was happening every day, regular as clockwork, between midday and 2 p.m. They were even able to take photographs as the fox came so close. She was probably a vixen with cubs needing the extra food, and popping over for a quick hot snack was so easy that it became a habit. After a week, we thought 'enough is enough', and it was hardly fair on the chickens being diminished by one daily; they must have almost got to the point of drawing lots to see who was to go next! Borrowing a gun from his brother-in-law, Derek took a packed lunch and sat in the chicken house. Watching through the window he lay in wait. It was a clear sunny day and he eventually saw her slip through the hedgerow at the far side of the homeground. He cocked the gun then so that the noise would not disturb her as she came nearer. Her lovely red body turned towards the orchard; taking just a few steps into the field, she stopped with one front leg up and sniffed the air, and then the ground, she was unsure. Pensive, she glided a few yards further; no, something was wrong and she swung herself round with a flash of her brush and disappeared back through the hedge from where she came. Silently relieved, Derek broke the barrel of the gun. She had not even come within the sights of the gun but she could smell danger. That vixen never came again during the day for a hot snack.

A couple of years later, we had contained the chickens in the large chicken house with a straw yard during the worst of the winter months. Spring was on its way and we had reverted to allowing them back out into the orchard during the day to scratch around. On that day, I was making my way to the chicken house to shut them up for the night and met up with Derek walking through the orchard to check on the sheep who were due to start lambing. Discussing the day's events, we walked out together and saw a ewe on her own away from the flock, usually a sure sign that she has or is about to lamb. We made our way to her and were pleased to see our first set of twins for the year. Picking the lambs up by their front legs, allowing them to hang either side of me, I carried them into the yard. It does not seem a comfortable way to carry them, but you should never carry newborn lambs against you because you are putting your scent on to them and the ewe could well reject them. The occasional bleat from the lambs encouraged the ewe to follow and Derek guided her from behind to get her indoors to a pen where she would be given a straw bed and some fresh hay and water. Derek usually brings his ewes and lambs in for the first night to protect them from the fox. After twenty-four hours the lambs are strong and can keep up with their mother, and very few are lost.

Safely ensconced in a warm shed, the ewe was grunting in a motherly fashion as the lambs, intent on suckling, searched under her belly to find the teats. Success was met by the frenzied shaking of their tails and slurping noises proved that this ewe had plenty of milk. Having satisfied their hunger, the lambs, still with the froth of milk round their mouths, skipped in the straw before settling close to the ewe, who was now lying by the hay chewing her cud. Standing watching over the half door, we both agreed that this was one of the times when farming seems worthwhile and you are at peace with the world. It was dark by now, and switching off the light in the shed we made our way back across the yard to go indoors. The end of another day – neither of us remembering that twice we had passed the chicken house and not even thought about shutting the door.

As dawn broke the next morning, the evidence of what we had not done was very clear before our eyes. The orchard looked as if it had been snowing. Feathers strewn across the grass everywhere, dead and dying chickens discarded, some not even eaten. Others with just the heads bitten off. Chickens, in a state of shock, cowered in corners and some had even died purely from asphyxiation: panic-stricken, they had fled into corners and piled on top of each other. Anger at what the foxes had done welled in both of us, thinking of the waste and of the pain that the chickens must have endured before being finally killed. But worst of all was the guilt, the knowledge that we had both been totally to blame for not shutting them up the previous day. Bad husbandry. Over fifty chicken carcasses were picked up and it cast a shadow over the whole day. 'If only . . .' was the phrase that ran through both our minds, and maybe it was a good thing that nobody asked us what we thought of foxes at that time. But you would expect a fox to take some chickens if a poultry door is forgotten . . .

I was up in London staying overnight with my mother. We had gone to see a show and were visiting the Ideal Home Exhibition the next day before returning home. As usual, I rang the farm to see if all was well. On speaking to Derek, and taking into account previous events, I think it showed the ultimate in love and devotion (I think to me) when he explained that acting on a call-out, he was now nursing a very small chocolate-brown bundle that needed to be fed every four hours as it was only three days old, and 'Thank God' I was coming home the next day so that I could nurse the tiny fox cub. I could not wait to see the new arrival as soon as I got home. Derek had managed wonderfully but was more than ready to pass the responsibility to me. He had never liked all the messing about with bottles, and this certainly had not changed his mind; and to have to feed a fox cub was very much against the grain! We called her Heidi, a sort of play on words seeing as I had been for a day at the Ideal Home, never realizing just how she was going to live up to that name. A farmer had been shooting foxes on his own land as he was having problems with them attacking his lambs. On checking that the last one he had shot was dead, he found that she had been carrying a small cub. He had no qualms about shooting the adult foxes as he needed to protect his sheep, but this little cub was not guilty of any attacks so he carried it home and contacted Derek who had collected her. She was absolutely beautiful, so small she fitted in the palm of my hand and, as she was only about three days old, her eyes were still closed. I wondered if anything so small could survive, but was not taking into account the tenacity of a fox cub. Wrapped in a warm towel, she warbled to show that her next feed was due. At that age, her fur was not really very long but the tell-tale white tip was to be seen at the end of her tail, tucked tightly against her body to retain the heat. We see so many animals go through the farm, but I knew that Heidi was going to be special.

The rate at which this little cub grew was phenomenal. By the end of the week her eyes were open, and pretty deep blue eyes looked back at us; another week and she had become a ball of fluff. She could wag her tail, maintain a very high-pitched warble until she gained the attention she required – she could also spit! Even at this age, when suddenly surprised by a noise or movement, her response was like lightning. We noticed that when she started to move around she carried one of her back legs and it was found that her hip was injured. Maybe she had damaged it as she fell when her mother was shot. Barry, our vet, gently examined her and said that it might correct itself but, if not, he would hopefully be able to operate and correct it. If operated on, she would need to be restricted for a few weeks and she would not be able to be released for some considerable time.

Compared to badger cubs, who do not open their eyes until five weeks of age and emerge from the sett only at eight weeks, it was obvious that the fox has to mature a lot faster in order to survive. Although Derek had only looked after her for the first couple of days, she had bonded to him and would greet him with such enthusiasm, flattening her ears and curving her small body as she trilled her welcome. This admiration was not mutual, and he did his best to ignore her. At three weeks, despite her back leg, she was quite agile and the fact that he was sitting trying to read a paper was no problem as her sharp little claws made it easy to scale the sides of the chair. Excited at being so close to him, she promptly urinated over his front which led to Derek leaping up and the fox cub catapulting across the room. Both the boys and I mustered all the control we could, looking mostly at the floor, doing our utmost not to laugh. Derek fled the room to change his jumper, slamming the door fiercely behind him; it only marginally missed Heidi's nose, who, concerned at seeing he was upset, had thought she would follow. We did our best from then on to steer her away from Derek, but anything she could find belonging to him was usually taken behind the chair and chewed, which led to a few problems in the weeks ahead. Both Simon and Daniel were very fond of Heidi and she spent a lot of the time in their bedrooms, and actually took over the toy cupboard on the landing between their two rooms as her sleeping place. By this time she was nearly two months old and as her hip had not corrected, Barry operated and she had to be restricted to the kitchen for a few weeks.

The bottom floor of the farmhouse is now used as a tearoom and we live in the top two floors, having a door at the top of the first staircase as the entrance to our private part of the house. So during the day, once her convalescence was over, as long as the door was kept shut Heidi was given the run of the rest of the house. A lot of time was spent playing with Barney or just sleeping. Often we would go upstairs to check that she was all right and call her name. If she was not hungry and was curled up somewhere warm, she just wouldn't bother to come. This would then lead to the horrible thought that maybe the door had been left open, and she may have slipped out. So we would start to look. It was like looking for a needle in a haystack. Foxes can move their bodies almost like fluid. The gaps and holes that they can get through are so small you would not believe it was possible. Foxes will very often adapt rabbit burrows for a home, and when these have been excavated it has been found that hardly any enlargement has been done to the tunnels as a fox can slip through such a small space. Sometimes Heidi was found in drawers, where they had just been left open a few inches, or behind furniture or fridges. In the end we gave up and knew that when she was hungry, the warbling noise would give her whereabouts away and she would run towards us, squirming on her tummy.

Derek has always loved cricket. It was something that he would have liked to have made a career out of but had never really been good enough. Nor had he been able to play village cricket as it is very much a sport that is played in the summer, when haymaking and milking had been far more important. So it was not until he was in his late thirties that he found he could organize his time off to play again. The fact that we had changed to making silage instead of hay meant that the summer work of storing food for the winter rations was done in a few days rather than a few weeks. So he goes to his cricket religiously each summer. His love is cricket and my love is wildlife. As long as I don't have to watch his cricket and he does not have to get too involved with the wildlife it suits us both! Each Saturday from May to September, he gets his kit and goes to a match and can forget about the farm for a short while. All the East Huntspill Cricket Team get on well together and, having a healthy sense of humour, often jibe each other quite a lot over incidents in their lives. If Derek is a few minutes late, it would probably be met with 'I suppose you've been walking a badger and it held you up' or 'Too busy saving the seagulls, were you Derek!' This he has learnt to live with.

Derek kept his kit in a sports bag under the bed and, as I have previously mentioned, Heidi had the run of the house. One week he must have left the bag open and Heidi found it.

The next Saturday, Derek went off as usual and amid all the banter got changed into his whites. Padded up, waiting to bat, he sat on the sidelines. The sun was shining gloriously and the team members who were not playing were sprawled on the grass watching the state of play. 'Ow's zat!' was the cry as the cricket ball was hurled at the stumps, knocking the bails in all directions, signalling that now was Derek's turn to face the ball. Picking up his bat, he tugged on his padded gloves (new that season!) to experience a soggy, mushy feel to his gloves which had not been there before; and pulled right on, a pink thumb pushed through the tattered and chewed mess of white leather. I was given to believe that his feelings were expressed quite explicitly, and on explaining the reason for the destruction of his gloves, quite a lot of ragging went on for the rest of the afternoon. Failing to comment on this slight nuisance that was being caused, I did feel that maybe he should have decided to keep his kit in a different place, especially when a few weeks later a similar incident happened as he pulled on his cricket sweater (quite a small hole really in the middle of the back), and even a repeat performance with a second pair of gloves (which I had dutifully replaced).

With her red coat coming through, Heidi's eyes were changing into a deep orange, and with her ears now pointed she was becoming a true fox. Heidi was completely weaned by the age of four weeks, and by this I mean that when given a piece of meat, there was no way that you were going to get it off her. Despite being reared on her own, the instinct to protect and fight for her food came naturally. Now was the time, in the wild, that the vixen would be bringing food back to the cubs and it would be survival of the fittest as to who got the most food.

We have a firm of window cleaners, who come every month and clean right through. Adrian, the boss, is a tall man with long blond hair, and is of the appearance that he could certainly look after himself if he ever needed to. He always cleans the windows inside the house and was warned of Heidi being upstairs. Adrian uses a shaggy chamois cleaner and a cloth for the windows, and he got half the way round upstairs without seeing Heidi. She was not far away. The shaggy chamois cleaner looked very much like the skin of an animal to her and, stalking him, she waited her chance. Having used the chamois, Adrian laid it on the windowsill as he changed to using the cloth. A red body launched itself from behind the chair, snatched the chamois, collided with the vase which she had misjudged and slid along the windowsill, anchoring her claws into Adrian's legs to stop herself from going any further. She misread Adrian's startled cry as danger and threw herself back from him, spitting and growling, to abate any thoughts that he may have had about retrieving his chamois. Standing back, Adrian saw her disappear down the hall dragging the shaggy trophy which was nearly twice her size. A very shocked man came downstairs, asking if it was possible to have his cleaning cloth back. Retrieving the cloth ended, even for me, in a blooded thumb and it was only by swapping a dead chick with her that she surrendered it to me in the first place. Adrian went back upstairs to finish his job – only to return ten minutes later as she had got it again! This time I threw a towel over her to reclaim the cloth and then shut her in the kitchen until Adrian had finished. A solitary howl sounded her disapproval.

Adrian and his mates are always interested in what we do and never know what to expect in any of the rooms. They were cleaning on the housing estate in Highbridge when, much to their horror, they saw a rat moving around the road. It looked to be ill but was still very much alive. They were worried as it would soon be time for the children to come out of school and they did not want to risk the chance of one of them trying to pick it up. 'Ring Pauline' was the decision. Mandy and I went to the estate armed with gloves and a carrying box. On arrival, the three brave men had caught this rat by overturning a dustbin on to the road where the rat was and had placed three large bricks on top in case he was related to Houdini. Having nothing to slide under the dustbin and thus keep him enclosed, Mandy and I decided to lift the side of the dustbin slowly as one of us tried to catch it. Needless to say, it ran through our hands and under a car. Three men disappeared, or at least stood a safe distance away. The rat, probably poisoned, was not moving all that fast so, sliding along each side of the car, we managed to catch it and place it in the carrying box. Standing up triumphant, we had saved the day. 'Eee,' said one of the window cleaners, 'You were as good as a pair of Jack Russells!' How's that for a compliment?

Luckily the rat died soon after we got home, which got us out of the ethical dilemma of whether we should try to save a rat or not, seeing as it is just another wild animal. Classed as vermin, do they deserve to be saved? But then the fox, grey squirrel and mink are vermin also.

With Heidi in the house and her scent glands growing stronger, Derek could have answered this question quite quickly on all counts! Foxes are almost impossible to house-train, and Heidi's favourite place of depositing her faeces was just at the top of the stairs as you came through to our part of the house. We all learnt to open the door carefully so not to spread any offending deposits that may have been left there! When I tell you how foxes will run up the chimney from the fireplace and along shelves to prove their agility you will begin to understand the reason why foxes are not considered as suitable pets. You may also think that Derek, by now, must have been halfway to deserving a halo. Most of the 'little things' that Heidi got up to were covered over as best we could before Derek found out about them. But even Derek was upset when it was discovered that someone had left the door open and Heidi was nowhere to be seen. We searched everywhere but to no avail. As she was often taken out for walks she did know the area, but how far she would go we did not know; and most of our neighbours shoot, so that was a worry as well. By bedtime she was still not to be seen. We had all walked different ways calling, desperate to hear her silly warbling call, but nothing. We decided to go to bed and leave the doors open right through the house and just hope that she would return.

I lay in bed listening for what seemed to be hours, but sleep eventually came: but I woke at 5 a.m. Being summer it was already daylight, and creeping silently from the bed without disturbing Derek, I made my way towards the boys' room. There lying in the toy cupboard on her back was Heidi. Too tired to move, she wagged her brush. Moved to tears, I fondled her head in a quiet welcome and then went and shut all the doors to return to bed for a couple of hours of sleep that would be far more peaceful than the previous ones.

Having had the pleasure of a night on the tiles. Heidi became quite adept at slipping through the door unnoticed, but each time she returned to her cupboard. It was, though, becoming increasingly difficult to keep her in the house and slowly we got her used to being in with Gordon and Bennet. They both took to her immediately. Once we were sure that both the boys were unsuitable to be released we had both of them neutered, as we felt it was unfair for them to have the urge to breed and not have their freedom. So Heidi joining them was no problem. To start with she was in with them for a few hours each day, until eventually she spent most of her time in with them and came into the house with us only now and again (mainly when Derek was out for the evening – followed by a spray of fresh air through the house to get rid of the evidence before he came home!). We often took her for a walk, and Mandy sometimes used to take her down on the beach with her dogs.

Heidi's hip improved in time and by the time she was a year old there was hardly any hint of a limp to be seen. By then we no longer had Bennet, and another fox came to us from a vet's. It was a young fox that had been caught in a snare and it had been necessary for the vet to amputate the back leg. Then infection broke out again and the vet had to amputate higher and spent a lot of time giving blood transfusions and medication to save her. Now on the mend, the thought was that she would not survive in the wild and so she came to us. What else could we call her but Tripod! As a wild-born fox, she was never really tame but would eventually come for her food and come quite close as long as you did not try to touch her.

Winter came and all three foxes had their dense winter coats. The time to see them was first thing in the morning when the frost had coated their pen in a crust of white, and they would stand quite oblivious to the cold with their red bodies in stark contrast. They really are beautiful creatures. I always think that frost accentuates the beauty of things. It shows the finer details. We have peacocks on the farm and they roost each night in a large horse-chestnut tree right by the foxes' pen. The sight of them roosting in the tree with their three-foot tails cascading from the branches on a frosty moonlit night is really breathtaking.

That winter Derek bought me a pair of white peacocks for Christmas, something I had always wanted. We put them in the aviary opposite the foxes' pen to get them used to their surroundings. They could see the other peacocks around the farm and where they roosted at night, and after a couple of months we hoped to let them out so that they could integrate with the other peafowl.

By this time Heidi was just coming up to two years of age. I never gave it a thought, but she must have been in prime breeding condition. One fateful morning we awoke to find a hole in the wire of the foxes' pen. The wire was double-sided, but we thought that probably a dog fox had come and chewed one side of the wire as Heidi chewed the other side. Both Heidi and Tripod were gone. Gordon, bless him, decided he was too old for life on the outside and preferred to have his food served up twice a day.

We never saw Heidi again. I am sure that she must have come to grief as she was so tame; even if she had paired, I think she would have returned, even just in the distance. Mandy was really grief-stricken; she had spent a lot of time with her and foxes are her favourite animal. We searched, put food out, let people know in case they found a friendly fox, but nothing was ever heard of her.

A week later, whoever learnt the art of chewing the wire returned and killed my white peacocks.

Tripod was another matter. She was sighted many times, and with the distinctive three legs she could not be mistaken. Shutting up the poultry two months later, I found that someone was beating me to it. There in the orchard was a fox with a large Brahma cockerel in its mouth. Shouting, I startled it and the fox dropped the cockerel and ran. A few yards away it stopped and turned before disappearing out of the gate. The fox had three legs. The cockerel suffered a severely bruised neck but survived to live another day. As did the guinea fowl in June. Peter, one of our morning cleaners, is one of those gems which every establishment hopes to have. He can mend anything. Not being very tall, Peter has to put up with all sorts of remarks about 'not realizing he was in because we couldn't see him over the counter!' but he takes it all very well. Living a very full life (to the despair of his wife) it is not unknown for Peter to be here still working at 11.30 at night, having been busy doing something else during the day. We are thinking of buying him a miner's lamp to wear on his head for night work! Anyway, it was Peter who early one morning was about to clean the Visitor Centre, and hearing a commotion from outside turned to see what all the fuss was about. Three guinea fowl hurtled round the corner followed by a three-legged fox with a mouthful of feathers. An unsuccessful Tripod. Seeing Peter in the yard, she decided not to carry the matter any further and slunk away. Talk about biting the hand that feeds! The depletion in the numbers of guinea fowl, peacocks and ducks (all the breeds that roost out or are on the pond) during the summer proved she was around quite close, although we mustn't blame it all on her as there are always a lot of foxes around here. At least it does show that three-legged foxes can sometimes survive in the wild.

We now have a fox called Amber to keep Gordon company, she is one that came from the RSPCA at the age of six months. When she was put into the large enclosure she never de-tamed, despite efforts on their part of chasing her away as they took in the food to try and make her wary of people. So it was a question of either putting her down or finding a home for her. Knowing Gordon was on his own, she was offered to us.

Not all stories of being called out to sick and injured animals have a happy ending. We were once called out to St John's School in Highbridge. They had seen a very dehydrated fox under the hedge at playtime and realized it needed medical attention, so Mandy and I went out with our equipment. It took some time to locate as, even though it was very ill, its fear of humans forced it to try and get away. Pathetically thin, this vixen was covered in flies' eggs ready to hasten her impending death. We took her straight through to the vet where we saw Colin. Keeping her head covered to lessen her fear, Colin soothed her by talking softly to her. Thoroughly examining her body he found a large cancerous growth which was in its final stages. Beyond help, quickly and quietly she was put to sleep and the pain that she had been experiencing came to an end as her body finally relaxed. Checking her once more, Colin looked at her teeth: 'A sad end,' he said, 'but to a long life. I would say she was at least 10 years old.'

The average life of a fox is two years because of the high fatality of youngsters. But once they have reached the age of three, they can go on to live a long time. This old lady had enjoyed a good life and, hopefully, we were able to make the end of her life a little easier for her.

7

Prickly Problems: Surprised by Hedgehogs

The hedgehog has been with us for millions of years and during this time has not adapted in any way. As I heard someone say at a lecture, 'If you get it right the first time, why bother to change?' Despite being persecuted and even eaten in the past, they can still be found in our countryside today. It is not until chance gives you the opportunity to meet a live hedgehog that you can appreciate how attractive it is.

It was during the first winter of being at the farm that, from the kitchen, I heard an incredibly loud scream. So loud, in fact, that on investigating I was sure it must have come from the yard. It was evening so the outside light was the only source of illumination to help find where the noise had come from. Sheena, our red setter, who had already been outside joined me to see what all the fuss was about. Standing still, I waited to see if the noise would be repeated. It had been such a blood-curdling scream that I could not just ignore it. Ears pricked, Sheena sat beside me, listening too. Looking up at me she could not understand why I was still just standing there. Not a great believer in loyalty, she decided to return to the backhouse rather than stand out on a cold windy night, and anyway, unbeknown to me, she had found something more interesting. Watching her trot back to the house, in the way that only setters can with her auburn feathered coat catching the breeze, I thought that perhaps she had the best idea, especially as in the rush I had dashed out without picking up a coat. Just a few more minutes, I thought, shivering, and I would go back in too. Only moments after her disappearance the scream came again and I immediately realized that it had come from the backhouse, and could well have something to do with Sheena.

Calling her, I rushed in and we both reached the back door at the same time. She had come out from the old dairy that was attached to the house, this time with ears down, looking very guilty, having got the distinct impression that she had done something wrong. What made her look even more comical was the two or three spines stuck well and truly to the bridge of her nose, which straight away explained that her confrontation had been with a hedgehog. Shutting her into the house, I quickly removed the spines and told her that any further first aid would have to wait! Reaching for a torch as there was no electricity in the dairy, I went to see what sort of state the other opponent was in. This was not going to be easy at all because, over the years, the dairy had been a dumping ground for almost everything and, although on my list of 'jobs to do', it was not one that I had tackled yet. This room was where the cheese used to be made many, many years ago, and the cheese vat and moulds with dairy equipment lay neglected on one side. An old wooden staircase leading up to the cheese room, where the cheeses used to be stored, was on one side and under this all the wellingtons – those in use, and those outgrown – were pushed out of the way. The boots in use, coated with mud from the day's work, look shiny compared to the rejected ones, now dusty and full of cobwebs. Further into the room, thrown-out implements, forgotten toys and fishing tackle all jumbled together made me think that to find a hedgehog in all this was going to be practically impossible. If I moved too much, there was the possibility that something would fall and injure it unknowingly anyway. It was going to be easier to let the Hedgehog Detective back out from the house and get her to find the victim.

Sheena obliged quite quickly, happy to prove the retriever instinct that we often said she never had. Too many times she had been sent after articles and on finding them picked them up, cheered on by us watching, only to drop them in all the excitement halfway back and return with nothing in her mouth, and completely confused as to what she went for in the first place! But this time she came up trumps. The sight of a hedgehog hopelessly tangled in the fishing tackle made me realize how easy it is for wildlife to get trapped in our everyday rubbish. On further inspection it was possible to see that one of its back legs had been trapped for some considerable time with fishing line which had bitten into the skin causing the limb to swell, and in the vain attempt to escape, the hedgehog had nearly amputated the leg. Guilt flooded into my emotions as I examined it further in the brighter light of the kitchen. If the tackle had been cleared away and stored properly, this would never had happened.

The animal was exhausted and past the point of curling up. Setting to work with scissors and tweezers, I cut away at the line that was tangled around the spines and carefully picked out the nylon thread that had been driven deep into the leg. When I had swabbed the little creature with disinfectant and powdered it for fleas, I made a makeshift pen by the Rayburn and hoped that the warmth would help it get over the shock of being handled and brought into a strange environment. Food and water were put down in the pen as well and, watching quietly from a distance, I was pleased to see her feed. She was so hungry and thirsty as she had probably been trapped for quite a few days. Only the interest of a red setter had frightened her so much that she had emitted the scream that hedgehogs are quite capable of, although one would never have believed that such volume could be achieved by such a small animal. Slowly the warmth had revived her, and her head poked out from her box, inquisitive as to her surroundings. We had shut all the cats and dogs out of the way, and could watch as her wet pointed nose sniffed the air, smelling the food not far away, and two shiny eyes surveyed the unusual territory. With ears twitching in the frill of hair that framed her face, the only sound she would probably have heard was the kettle slowly simmering on the Rayburn. The smell of the food was too inviting to worry about the strange surroundings and she lifted herself to move towards the dish, her body gaunt from having to survive on her stored fat whilst she had been trapped. Dragging her injured leg, she reached her food and when full, returned to her box to sleep. That was as much as I could do for the night but tomorrow it would be off to the vet.

Hedgehogs are one of the three mammals in the British Isles that actually hibernate. The other two are bats and dormice. They store fat in their bodies in the months leading up to the cold winter, and then, once the weather turns cold and food is difficult to find, they make a dry nest and go to sleep. Hibernation is a physical process where the body temperature is reduced to equal that of its cold surroundings, thus saving energy, and the heartbeat reduces also, slowing the breathing pattern at the same time. During this time the animal will live off the fat that has been stored. They do wake up at different times, and will sometimes leave their nest for another one particularly if disturbed or if the weather turns unusually warm for a period of time, causing them to arouse. I expect, knowing our wet surroundings, this hedgehog had probably been flooded out and had come into the backhouse looking for somewhere dry to sleep. If she had been undiscovered by the dog, eventually she would have died. So many birds and mammals die from the carelessness that we are all guilty of, at some time or another.

The next morning we were pleased to find that Lulu (so named due to her close resemblance to a loo brush) had survived the night. A vet's appointment was made, not only for Lulu but also for Sheena who was sporting a very red and angry rash on her nose. In all the excitement, her first aid on the previous night had been forgotten about! The vet immediately recognized the problem that Sheena had – evidently they get quite a few dogs with infected noses through having attempted to roll a hedgehog around. Treating the hedgehog was not to be quite so simple. Lulu had begun to feel better and was now quite capable of rolling into a ball. Fortunately the injured leg was so swollen that it was impossible for her to tuck it in, so the vet was presented with a complete prickly ball with one leg sticking out, almost giving the appearance of a handle. As this was the part of the anatomy that required attention it did not matter too much, but we left without the vet ever seeing her face. The leg unfortunately had to be amputated, but the line had bitten in so deep there was hardly any need to cut much of it away. Having cleaned it up and dusted the wound, the vet said that it should heal over quite easily and there was enough of a stump for her to lead a normal life, but that it would be best to keep Lulu for a while, to build up strength, before finally releasing her. He noticed that she snuffled, so gave me some antibiotics to clear it up and asked us to bring her back in a week.

Back home, Lulu relaxed and was glad to be back in her pen. The children thought she was lovely and enjoyed the period of time that she was with us. She got so used to being picked up, so that we could clean her pen, that eventually she made no effort to curl up and could be handled quite easily as she kept her spines flat.

Her leg healed quickly and it was a much healthier and heavier hedgehog that returned to the vet the following week. The only problem was that the antibiotics had not cleared up the snuffles. The vet was very pleased with her apart from this, and thought that maybe Lulu had just not responded to that kind of antibiotic and gave me something different. As long as she responded to those, there was no need for him to see her again. (Sheena's nose, by the way, was back to normal!)

As we were passing the RSPCA'S Wildlife Centre a few days later we called in to see Colin Seddon for some advice on keeping Lulu until she was released. We have always been given a lot of support by the RSPCA who have readily given information and guidance on many occasions. 'Come and have a look at my ginger hedgehogs!', he said, and we followed him through to the pen. There snuggled in the corner was a 'mum' hedgehog and at least four or five tiny babies, all an unusual ginger colour. 'You don't see them that colour very often', Colin said. As I turned to go out, something caught my attention. Listening carefully, I said to Colin, 'Your hedgehogs have got the snuffles too.' 'What, that noise?', he said, pausing; 'They always make that noise.' Laughing, we told Colin how our vet, for the past two weeks, had been trying to cure Lulu of the symptoms. It certainly explained why she had not responded to the antibiotics!

We did tell our vet the outcome so that he did not treat any more 'sick' hedgehogs. This is very often the case with wildlife, that vets rarely come into contact with them and can sometimes misconstrue how an animal behaves. Certainly, if you find a good vet who is interested in wildlife, like the vets that we now use, they are worth their weight in gold. Our vets will strive to do whatever they can to treat what we take into them, with the proviso that after recuperation the animals will have quality of life and, in general, be released back into the wild.

We kept Lulu through to the spring. By now, when she had her evening exercise around the kitchen, she was using her stump as naturally as a leg; and indeed, if you did not know the foot was missing, it was impossible to tell. Watching her scrabble over things, you could appreciate what climbers hedgehogs can be and hence the funny stories of the many places they have been found. Many unfortunately die under cattle grids and in ponds where, having fallen in, they are unable to climb out. Just a plank strategically placed from top to bottom with not too steep an incline inside pits, or sloping sides built into a pond, can save many lives. Hedgehogs can swim but need to put their feet on something solid in shallow water to climb back out on to dry land.

When spring arrived, Lulu was placed in a hutch under a hedge with a run in front and kept confined for a couple of weeks so that she could get to know her surroundings once more. Then the run was taken away, although we still left food for her in the same place. She only stayed in the hutch for a week or so and then must have found a more desirable residence. It was later in the summer that, returning from a night out, we drove into the yard and startled a mother hedgehog crossing the yard with five tiny pin cushions scurrying behind her. Was it Lulu? We like to think so.

As I have said before, the agility of hedgehogs can lead them into trouble, and we have on several occasions had them brought in covered in oil having fallen into containers or car pits. One particularly bad case was one that had fallen into a drum of tractor oil; on arrival he was the stickiest mess I have ever seen. The main health hazard is how much oil the animal has swallowed; a good dose of koagel helps to remedy this problem if it is not too severe. However, being given by mouth to an uncooperative hedgehog, it is not the easiest of procedures to carry out! Esso, as he was aptly named, was no exception to the rule and was going to beat the world record of how long a hedgehog can remain curled up. He was a big hedgehog, too. After rocking him gently to and fro, which usually does the trick of uncurling them, we decided the best thing to do was to give him his first bath. With Esso placed on the draining board, still tightly curled, I ran a bowl of warm soapy water. Briefly the nose extended from the sticky mess, only to retract immediately on my approach. Warning him that he was going in the water, I placed him into the soap suds and his head immediately appeared – obviously, he had decided it was better to uncurl rather than drown. Taking advantage of the opportunity, Mandy, who is in charge of our animal care, syringed the koagel into his mouth and we were winning. Working the soapy water into his spines with a paint brush took quite some time; this was followed by a warm shower. Esso had five baths over the next two weeks, alternating between washing-up liquid and swarfega, which he hated. Having placed him on the draining board, you only had to start to run water and the tightly curled ball would spring into life and scrabble to get away. I'm sure he had a phobia about water for the rest of his life. Having gained weight after eating us out of house and home, eventually, with a clean coat in such good condition that he would be the envy of any male hog, Esso returned to his owner to be released back where he came from. His owner had safely disposed of the oil, and now aware of the hazards of open containers, had said he would be taking more care in the future.

We have hedgehogs of all ages brought into us, right from the smallest when they are only a few days old. When first born the baby hedgehog is pink and blind and the spines are covered by skin. The spines shoot through very quickly after they are born, but are white and soft, the babies needing no protection as they are usually born into a specially made nest. The first spines are very sparse and the skin is quite visible, but brown spines soon grow until eventually, when fully grown, an adult will have an estimated 5,000 spines (but I'm not sure who had the patience to count them!).

These spines will moult and regrow independently like the hair

. . . soapy water into his spines with a paint brush . . .

on our head so at no time should you get a balding hedgehog. After fourteen days their eyes open, and by the time they are four weeks old the youngsters are weaning and will soon be out foraging under the close eye of their mother. At the age of six to seven weeks the family starts to disperse and they start to lead the solitary life characteristic of the hedgehog (apart from during the breeding season!).

Most hedgehog babies are born from late May onwards so orphans are brought in from that time, for varying reasons. Sometimes a nest is inadvertently dug up, or moving of rubbish destroys the nest; but there is a higher number in the autumn when late babies are born and the mother deserts the nest, knowing there is not enough time for the babies to reach a weight that will enable them to survive the winter. Driven by hunger, babies will leave the nest in search of food and their plaintive cries soon attract attention. Similarly, young hedgehogs are found wandering in early winter unable to find food, but knowing they have not enough stored fat to hibernate; they will eventually die if not helped. A hedgehog must weigh at least 1 lb(450 g) to be able to survive the winter.

It was in August, our busiest time of year for visitors, that three very tiny babies came into us, still with their eyes shut. When clearing rubbish from a corner, a lady intent on getting her garden tidier noticed that the last shovelful of rubbish she had thrown on to the wheelbarrow was beginning to move. Horrified, she stood, praying it was not a grass snake, as the bundle slid from the pile of debris and burst open to reveal a squealing mass of tiny hedgehogs. Relieved that it hadn't been a snake, she fetched an old shoebox and placed the babies on an old towel inside. She then realized that she had another problem: what to do with them? Then she remembered New Road Farm and, a telephone call later, we were on our way to collect them. It sometimes happens that, if the babies are placed with the original nesting back near where they came from, the mother may return and move them to another safe place; but, as they had been handled and so much of the area had been destroyed, this was hardly likely. Besides, being so young, the babies would have had trouble in keeping their body temperatures high enough to survive until the mother returned.

I automatically fall back into the routine of the feeds being little and often; with three mouths to feed, you can never hurry these things. When so small, babies like these need to be wiped to empty bladder and bowels before feeding and I usually dust a little bit of baby powder on them to stop the skin from chapping. I was being watched by a visitor one day, who remarked jokingly that there would not be baby wipes and powder in the wild. 'No,' I quipped, 'but their mother would lick them clean in the wild, and I'm not prepared to go that far!'

Anyone working with animals will know that things usually happen together. On the same day, a late telephone call at 10 p.m. described a family of hedgehogs that were in a garage. The owner knew they were there and had been monitoring their progress. Each night 'mum hedgehog' would go out and forage and was always back with her babies the following morning, but not that morning; and frequent checks throughout the day showed that she had not returned at all. They were worried she may have been run over. Now the babies were hungry and crying, could they bring them in to us to look after? Another five babies soon arrived, and when my late night feed was finished, I had three babies tucked up in one box and another five in a box next to them. Kept warm by an infra-red lamp, they were snuggled under a blanket. It is surprising just how warm you must keep hedgehog babies for them to survive. A temperature of at least 25 degrees Celsius or 75 to 80 degrees Fahrenheit is necessary for them to stay healthy. By the time I was halfway through the next day, the hedgehog babies had grown used to my smell, which they related to, and no sooner had I started to feed one tiny baby than a chorus of impatient cries would start up. They could not see why my milk bar could not accommodate them all at the same time, just as their mum had, but I am afraid they just had to wait their turn.

Although these babies were just beginning to turn grey they still had the very wrinkled faces which, together with their newly grown spines, made them look like miniature old men with punk rocker hairstyles. Holding each one in turn on its back, with my thumb placed between their front legs, they would paddle with their paws in the same way as they would against their mother to stimulate the flow of the milk. Sometimes, when you place young hedgehogs on to something that smells different from their usual surroundings, they will anoint themselves. Throwing their heads back over their body, they exude a frothy kind of saliva which they spread over their spines. This is part of the normal behaviour of a hedgehog and no one has really been able to find out the reason why they do it. Certainly, ones that we have had will carry on for a few minutes and then forget all about it. The contortion of the body in the effort to reach their backs with this kind of spittle would startle anyone unaware that this behaviour is quite natural.

Eight babies took quite a lot of time to feed and I was pleased the next morning when a telephone call came from the people who owned the garage, to say that 'mum' hedgehog had returned and was back in her nest. I asked them to bring her out to the farm and we would try and introduce the babies back to her. There were two problems we were likely to experience. One was rejection, either by the mother now that the babies smelt of me, or the babies rejecting the mother now that they were used to me feeding them. The other problem was dietary; having adapted from their mother's milk to the substitute milk, we were now expecting them to change back again to the mother's milk. When the 'mum' hedgehog arrived, you could not have met a more disgruntled hog. Bristling and spitting, she made it quite plain she did not agree with all this upheaval. Still, taking into account that she must have been trapped somewhere for a couple of days, had arrived home to find all her babies gone, and finally to be scooped up into a box and driven in one of those terrible things that frequently squash her relatives, it would have been hardly surprising if she had needed psychiatric care!

We put her in a box with a nest of hay and a small run lined with newspapers, and once she had settled in the hay we quietly introduced the babies. With complete disdain, the 'mum' pulled the hay from underneath the babies, hauled it over on top of the food dishes (of course) and made a fresh nest just for herself, leaving the babies to squirm around on just the newspaper. It is never a good idea to act too quickly where nature is concerned, so refraining from the urge to pick them up and take them away, I left them for a while to see what would happen. Each baby in turn crawled what must have seemed to be a tremendously long way, only to face the next problem of desperately trying to scale the mound of hay to get back to their mother, whom they had obviously recognized. With itching fingers, I watched, dying to help. Sometimes tumbling back, each one eventually reached the side of their mother and stuck their nose underneath her spiky coat. No rapturous welcome, just a shake of her body to help accommodate each sibling was all the emotion the mother would show. With fingers now crossed, I left them to it. When I looked in on them later, all that could be heard was the contented snoring of a happy family. We watched the droppings from the family for the next few days, and as all was normal, they were moved to an outside pen. They were kept for two months and then all released to their home territory.

With my hog family reduced back to just three life was quite a bit easier, and when they were big enough we put them in to the nocturnal house until release sites were found for them. It was during this time that we noticed that two of the young lads working for us, Clynton and Lee, would, if possible, evade the job of cleaning out and feeding the hedgehogs. Perhaps they did not like the smell as hedgehogs are not the cleanest of animals, as many people attempting to keep them have found out to their expense; or maybe they were squeamish at cutting up the dead chicks which were sometimes mixed in with their food. Mystified, I eventually asked Clynton and Lee outright just what was it that they did not like? The answer was that, well, they spit and hiss and – would you credit it? – these strapping young teenagers were frightened of them. Just what injuries they had thought that these huge animals, which can reach all the way up to the ankle, would inflict does not bear thinking about. These 'cowardly' lads that we employ were quite pleased when eventually the triplets were released and the teasing stopped.

We do not usually release hedgehogs on the farm because of the badgers. People often offer to home a hedgehog and we then check to see that their garden will have a good food supply for the animal. Their main diet is beetles, caterpillars and earthworms but they will also eat slugs, snails and insects so they really are a gardener's friend. Maybe with a hedgehog on 'duty', it will not be necessary to use all those garden chemicals, particularly as it can never be proved just how much of a detrimental effect it has on the mammals and birds that visit. Hedgehogs require cover and plenty of areas where they can build their nests and be undisturbed but the gardens must also allow them to escape to other areas, although it is always hoped that they will stay or at least visit the garden they are released from. The 'foster parents' must not be too tidy and clear away all the dead leaves and natural debris which will make good nesting material. Put first in a box in a suitable area, with a run to keep them secure, the hedgehogs are given a couple of weeks to get used to their surroundings; then the run is lifted, allowing them their final freedom, but with food still put down in the same place to support them until they can forage enough to be self-sufficient. Hopefully they will be around for the rest of their lives which, on average, is only two years, but many live to four or five and some are even known to have reached ten years.

The defence of rolling into a ball seems to work on many occasions. It has in fact been proved that, although it seems a silly thing to do when crossing a road with a car coming towards you, taking into account the speed of the vehicle and the chance of being missed by the tyres, there is a higher chance of survival by doing just that. Certainly as a deterrent to predators, it usually works – even those large human beings are loath to pick one up. Foxes are said to urinate on hedgehogs to make them uncurl and thus vulnerable, although I have yet to prove this! But a badger, with those lovely long powerful claws, has all the equipment to uncurl and even digest a hedgehog leaving the spiky skin completely intact, and these are sometimes found as the incriminating evidence. Many a badger lover has changed their allegiance on seeing 'their' hedgehog consumed by a passing badger. I hasten to add that hedgehogs are not part of a badger's staple diet, merely chance victims.

People who have visiting hedgehogs often worry about putting milk and bread out for them, having heard that it is not good for them. If they were fed completely on this diet, I could imagine that so much cholesterol would be detrimental to their health, but offered as a titbit with the wide variety of alternatives to be found in their own surroundings, I cannot see it doing too much harm. In fact, I reckon a little bit of what you fancy does you good. However, we do use goat's milk, not cow's, to rear our orphans, as the different fat content of cow's milk can upset young stomachs.

Whenever you show an animal to people, you will usually be asked: 'Do they bite?' When the animal in question had been a hedgehog, I had always replied, 'No'. I had a very attentive group of schoolchildren, out for the day to the farm, who were in the classroom in the Visitor Centre, talking about all the different animals that we kept and that could be found on a farm. A temporary guest at that time was a young hedgehog, which I had taken over to show the children, as so few children have seen a live hedgehog. As I walked along the rows of seats, so that the children could get a good look at it, one young girl wiggled a finger at the hedgehog; looking at it from the hedgehog's point of view, it must have appeared a rather nice juicy worm, which, if not caught, would probably disappear quite quickly. With a scream, the young girl made it absolutely clear that she had been bitten. Apologizing profusely, I guided her to the office where the First Aid box was kept; blood was streaming down her hand even though it had only been a nip. Stemming the flow of blood with some clean lint, I tried to tell the young girl just how lucky she had been to be bitten by a hedgehog, because I, certainly, did not know of anyone else who had. She was not impressed. So now, if I am asked if a hedgehog bites, I'm afraid the answer has to be – 'Yes!'

8

I've Lost My Mum: Orphans' Tales

There was a knock on the back door. Wondering who it might be, I left the tea cloth by the remaining washing up, and went to answer it. Shooing the barking dogs back indoors, I shut the door behind me. A young boy and girl, both aged around seven or eight, stood there, carefully holding a small cardboard box. Behind them, their bicycles had been thrown down at the foot of the steps and the wheels were still spinning from the urgent journey. I could see from the tear-stained face of the young girl that there had been a calamity and gently asked if there was anything I could do. In a faltering voice, the young girl explained that their cat had caught a mouse and although they had managed to take the mouse away, it did not look very well. Moving over to the bench seat in the backhouse, they offered the box for me to see the contents. There, wrapped carefully in some cotton wool, was the tiny body of a mouse and I could see straight away that, rather than a case of first aid, to see any improvement in its condition was going to require the art of resurrection (one qualification I don't have!). Taking the little mouse out of the box, I told them that unfortunately the shock had been too much for him and he had died. They must not blame the cat, I explained, because he was only doing what it is natural for him to do. I asked them where they had come from, as we live at least a mile from the village.

They said they were from East Huntspill and had heard that we looked after animals, and indeed, now I came to think about it, I did recognize their faces. Our children were now nearly grown up and it is surprising how out of touch you become with the villagers once your involvement with the local school ends. They seemed a little bit brighter, and I told them how good they were to have bothered to come so far on their bikes for the sake of a mouse. Leading them out to the shop, which was still unlocked, I offered the children a bar of chocolate each before they started their way home. Promising to bury the mouse in the garden, I waved goodbye to them as they cycled off, now having come to terms with the catastrophe that had beset them. With trowel in hand, I allotted the plot for the mouse and he was duly interred in the front garden and I resumed the washing up.

The next day, at around the same time, another knock came at the door and I found the same two children with yet another box held carefully in their hands. The cat had been at it again, they told me. This time the casualty was a small sparrow, in the same condition as the mouse, and I had the feeling that maybe the emotional upset was being put on; but as usual, giving in to the element of doubt, I consoled them. However, I felt quite convinced that my gut feeling had been right when, two chocolate bars later, they cycled madly away waving goodbye. The sparrow was laid to rest next to the mouse.

The following day, the half-expected knock on the door duly came and I was amused to see my two angels of care once again at my door, complete with box. One can only admire such business acumen in ones so young who, after the first tragic incident, realized this as a means of obtaining sweets, not to mention their ingenuity in finding dead animals once out from school to bring up to me. This last specimen was by no means fresh and it was obviously becoming more difficult to find suitable subjects. I explained that it really was such a long way to keep coming, and I just could not do anything to help if the animal was already dead. Minus two chocolate bars, they made their way home, and either the realization that they had been rumbled, or, maybe, the lack of dead animals, was the reason they did not return again.

Last summer, someone kindly brought me in a complete pickle jar of tiny mice that had been inadvertently disturbed when the shed was being cleared out. The nest had obviously had several families in it as the mice varied from transparent pink and blind little forms to grey babies whose fur was just coming through. There were twenty-seven in all! When tackling anything quite so small, the main problem is to find a feeder that is tiny enough for them to cope with; I have found that the easiest thing to use in these cases are the finest artist paint brushes that you can get. Fed on goat's milk, little and often, it is surprising how they will thrive. The first night, I did the last feed just before midnight, and although not fed again until seven the next morning, they all survived. Why bother, I'm sure many of you are saying, but then who's to say which life is more important? Even though mice are in the lower part of the food chain, they all have their part to play. The nicest thing with animals so small is that they mature very quickly and within a couple of weeks are off your hands.

Dealing with an ever-increasing variety of animals. I felt I needed to know a lot more about wildlife in general. Through joining the Somerset Trust Badger Group I came to know Doug Woods, a retired butcher, and his wife Olive. Doug has had a fervent interest in wildlife, particularly mammals, since he was a young boy and his knowledge is endless. Olive, in her own quiet way, can match his knowledge and enjoys prompting him when he is giving lectures and forgets a name or a statistic. Their love of the countryside has been passed on to their son, Michael, now a wildlife expert in his own right and freelance writer. To go on an early morning walk or a badger watch with Doug, quietly in the countryside, is a fascinating experience.

The first time I went, my son Simon and Mandy came with me. Having arranged to meet Doug at 5 a.m. by the woods, I set my alarm the previous night for 4.15 a.m. Derek, having heard our arrangements, thought we were completely mad – and I must admit, when the alarm went off, I was beginning to agree with him. Although it was June, it was still dark. Slipping out of bed, so as not to disturb Derek, I called the others and soon we were travelling along the empty road towards the Mendip Hills. Arriving by the woods, I parked and switched the lights off. The red glow of dawn was beginning to rise in the distance but at that particular time we were the only ones there. Did I have the right day? Or even the right time? But I need not have worried as soon Doug's car swung round into the car park and we got out of our car. It may have been summer, but at that time in the morning there was a chill to the air and I was glad of my heavy coat. The skyline was becoming lighter and, as if on demand, as we prepared for our walk, a tawny owl flew across to a large tree by the cottage on the edge of the wood and called to its mate, which we could see clearly perched on the opposite side. There was no traffic to be heard, just the mellow hooting echoing in the dewy morning. The strong smell of wild garlic drifted from the wooded banks as we made our way through the wooden gate. Startled by our presence, first one owl and then the other took off through the trees, probably back to their daytime roost, to digest what they had managed to catch that night and, unnoticed, to watch people like ourselves, who frequent their wood during the day. The sun was rising and the early morning chorus began. Identifying each bird, Doug was able to point out different ones so that we were able to locate where they were and listen to them singing heartily, partly to greet the new day and partly to lay claim to their territory.

Further up the path, Doug showed us a bedding trail, where a badger had been taking bedding back to its sett. Gathering a bundle of dry grass and leaves under their chins, badgers shuffle backwards, dragging the bedding back to their chambers. They will repeat this process over and over again, particularly if there is a good source of bedding, and small pieces get left behind as they move backwards, leaving a definite trail as evidence of their hard work. Following the trail, we found the sett with its typical D-shaped entrance, with a huge spoil heap outside made with all the excavated soil. The morning was warming up, but sometimes in the winter the warm moisture from the sleeping badger can be seen in the cold air, and on occasions even snoring can be heard! Leaving the badger in peace, we continued on our way.

The loud cawing of the rooks wheeling overhead nearly drowned the sound of the woodpecker about his business. A crash of leaves startled us: as we looked up, a grey squirrel scolded us for our intrusion. High in the fork of the tree, its drey looked like a heap of dry leaves, belying the art of carefully weaving the leaves and twigs, while still green and supple, that was its creation. Making us stop, Doug told us to use our noses, and the pungent smell that we all noticed was evidence that a fox had been by; footprints found close by a muddy puddle confirmed that we were right. The sun started to stream through the leaves and I no longer needed my coat. It was going to be a lovely day, but it was still very early and only the hum of a distant milking machine told us we were not the only ones about at that time in the morning. Coming out into a clearing, we noticed scrapings in the ground and the 'currant' droppings that were the tell-tale signs of rabbits; and as we moved further forward, disturbing their early morning feed, groups of them fled undercover, flashing their white tails as a warning to the others. Taking us over to some bushes, Doug showed us parts of the stems that had been chewed, leaving a jagged edge. This was a sign of deer browsing. Because they have no upper teeth, just a hard pad, they grip the stem and tear the ends off. Looking at the bushes, you could see how the lower growth was kept in check by constant browsing by the deer, but once above the reach of them, the bushes spread out, an odd effect that gives the appearance of topiary.

Having walked a circular route, all too soon we were back at the car park. Just as we crossed the last part of the field, Doug excitedly pointed to a bird flying over towards the hills. With its fluttering flight, we could tell it was a cuckoo. Arriving in this country in April, their call is the start of the summer; they find a suitable nest to lay their eggs in June, and fly back to Africa in July. The young, raised by foster parents, fly to Africa later in the season. Once fending for themselves, young cuckoos fatten quickly by eating a lot of hairy caterpillars. All other birds leave these alone as the hairs are an irritant to their digestion, but cuckoos can create balls of the hair and regurgitate them, in the same way as birds of prey bring up their pellets, and thus are able to feed on this otherwise neglected food source. When they are fully fit for the journey, and by some inbuilt instinct, they are able to travel all the way to Africa with no parents to guide them. Cuckoos lay eggs that match those of the bird in whose nest they were reared, and this determines where they in turn will lay their eggs. Hence a cuckoo reared by a blackbird will lay a blue egg: the same as a blackbird, so she must find a nest belonging to a blackbird to lay her egg; likewise, one reared by a robin must find a robin's nest to place her egg. Thanking Doug, we bade our farewells and returned home. Gloating that we had been up since 4 a.m., we treated ourselves to a cooked breakfast and talked over the experiences of the morning.

I have seen and heard Doug capture the atmosphere of these walks and enchant people with his lectures. I certainly never tire of hearing him. Sometimes I feel almost ashamed, knowing that there is so much around us that goes unnoticed, as unfortunately most of us are too busy with our lives even to be aware of its existence.

I have also, on many occasions, been badger-watching with

Doug. This is a question of wearing dark clothing that does not rustle, being taken to a sett, about half an hour before the time the badgers are known to emerge, and sitting very patiently and very quietly to see if they come out. Doug has particular setts that he regularly puts food down by, to encourage the badgers to forage there. Once the badgers are out, you stay rooted to the spot until the badgers move off to forage further afield. On my first watch with Doug, we saw eleven badgers. It was quite magical, almost as if you were intruding, to watch them play and preen, all of which is very much part of their social behaviour. A roe deer walked past after an hour, so as you can imagine, it was a watch that will take some beating.

Derek was intrigued at this interest in badger-watching, because although I have badgers here I find it fascinating to watch them in their typical habitat. One evening he decided to come along. Doug had arranged to meet six other people at the agreed spot and two of them unfortunately were late. This causes problems as it is important to get settled in your places before the badgers come out. We all waited. The four who had turned up were getting on in years, and as it was some way up to the sett, Doug decided to make a move. I offered to stay behind with Derek for a few more minutes, in case the other two arrived, and we would then follow on. Derek was still not over-keen on the idea of badger-watching, and so while we were waiting, I used my female persuasion and said we could go for a nice meal after the watch: this idea went down well. Luckily the two late arrivals turned up and we quickly made our way towards the sett. It was a young couple who turned up, one being a very attractive lady.

Walking quickly we followed the footpath, then climbed through a barbed-wire fence and scaled the wooded side of the cliff – not an easy task at the best of times, and made even trickier by the fact that we were in a hurry and that recent rain had made the going underfoot quite slippery. Nearing the site, we could see that Doug and the other four were already positioned, and I could tell by the signals from Doug that some badgers were already out. The young couple decided to scale a nearby tree, and Derek followed. (Did this have anything to do with the attractive female?) I made my way over to the other group. The noise of our arrival made those animals that were out run back underground. Everyone was quiet. Twenty minutes later a black and white head emerged, followed by another and then another.

Everyone was thrilled; but Derek, having sat in a tree for the last half an hour, was beginning to wonder how much longer this was going to go on. The badgers snuffled around, finding the peanuts and bacon scraps that had been scattered around for them. Glad to be above ground, they charged each other and played before settling to groom by scratching with their long claws and nibbling with their teeth. For once they did not seem to be in any hurry to move away. With the light now nearly completely gone it was difficult to see the badgers (or anything else for that matter), but I could almost feel the vibes being sent over from the tree that enough was enough. Eventually Doug decided that they had gone and we all rose stiffly from our positions to be joined by the 'roosters', two of whom were enthralled by the proceedings. We still had to remain as quiet as possible, and the next task was to get back to the cars. It was now nearly completely dark. No one had a torch and, as I mentioned before, some of the group were senior members and not very athletic. It was decided that we were all to hold hands, so as not to lose each other as we gingerly made our way down. I was next to Doug and Derek was following right at the end of the washing line.

Murmuring to Doug this was all an excuse for him to hold my hand, he softly confided in me that he had got me to be next to him because, as it was so dark, he was not sure of the way down and hoped that I could remember! It took us a long time, but following the lights of the local quarry we were eventually able to find our way back to the car. Needless to say, Derek has not been badger-watching again; and to rub salt into the wound, by the time we got back to the car it was too late to get a meal anywhere. I have a very understanding husband!

It was about twelve years ago that Doug realized that he had never seen a common dormouse. Knowing that they needed bramble, hazel and honeysuckle, all of which were present in woods on the Mendip Hills near where he lived, he decided to do some study work of his own. Starting with feeding tables, where you look for specific droppings, but which proved to be unsuccessful, he decided to put up nesting boxes. He placed 150 boxes in woods in the locality and immediately had a take-up of 25 per cent. With constant monitoring, Doug built up several years of records. Dr Pat Morris came to the area to lecture on dormice and stayed with Doug. Dr Morris, who is better known for his books on hedgehogs, monitors released hedgehogs in connection with the

. . . enough was enough . . .

RSPCA, to find out how they adjust to life in the wild after a time of captivity, and to prove just how successful the rehabilitation is for hedgehogs and what the best methods are.

During his stay, Doug offered to show him the local countryside. Dr Morris was keen to see the dormouse nestboxes and also looked at Doug's records. Surprised by the amount of success that Doug had had, Dr Morris set about obtaining a grant so that work could be increased; eventually Paul Bright, a graduate who had received his degree in Zoology, was taken on to assist with the monitoring and record-keeping, which was becoming increasingly valuable as more was being found out about the lifestyle of this small animal. Paul has since gained a doctorate and continues his work involved with the dormice from Bristol University.

Now a protected species, much more is known about the dormouse which is a secretive creature. Strictly nocturnal, it is also very shy, spending most of its time in the branches of trees. The dormouse is therefore difficult to find and is only rarely subject to predation. Living anything up to five years in the wild, its life is much longer than that of other small mammals and so it does not need to breed so readily. They will usually have only one or two litters a year, producing an average of four babies in each litter.

Dormice are a lovely golden colour with a long furry tail and, in size and appearance, are fairly similar to hamsters. Indeed, many years ago, before hamsters were brought into this country, when hedges were still laid by hand, workers would often find dormice which would be given to young boys for pets; the lads often carried them around in their pockets and even took them to school!

When food is hard to find or the weather becomes colder, dormice are able to go into a torpor to conserve their energy, much as bats do. As winter draws in, they almost double their body weight by storing fats, sometimes in a period of only three to four weeks. Then by reducing their body temperature to match that of their natural surroundings, they hibernate and sleep through the cold winter months, waking in the spring when their first food supply of pollen is available to them. It is estimated that they can be asleep for 75 per cent of the year. Remember the sleepy dormouse in the story book *Alice's Adventures in Wonderland*?

It was always thought that dormice hibernated in the base of the hedgerow; however, research carried out by fitting miniature radio collars on to them has revealed that they make a ball of moss and sleep in a crevice or hollow in the ground. The loss of ancient woodland, and the fact that hardly any coppicing is done now, which created the sprawling branches necessary for their habitat, has meant that their numbers have declined dramatically. Michael Woods has fifty nesting boxes that he monitors, in the woods at the back of his house. It was near one of these boxes that their family cat seemed intrigued with something in the branches. Michael's son Johnathon noticed the disturbance and went to investigate. The cat by then had caught a baby dormouse, which luckily Johnathon managed to retrieve. Looking into the nearby next box, he found five other small babies huddled together and a female dormouse that had been dead for quite some time. The babies were beginning to get very hungry and one had ventured outside to find food, but instead had found the cat. Johnathon collected them all up and took them indoors.

The next problem was what to do with them. Doug contacted me and asked if I would try to rear them. Normally, you cannot keep them unless you have a special licence, which Doug holds, but for welfare purposes this can sometimes be waived. When he arrived with the little family, I peeped into the box and lifted them out. They were no bigger than the tips of my fingers. With fine claws to each foot, they seemed to stick to your hands and it was quite difficult to unclasp them and put them back in their nest box. I had a glass tank ready for them with some small branches placed in it. When they climbed about on the branches you could see that they had special joints to their feet, adapted to help them grip the small twigs of the bushes they would usually live in. We weighed them before we put them into their new home: the smallest baby was only 3.5 grams, the largest 4.5 grams.

So little is known about the diet of dormice that I had a bit of a problem on my hands. The RSPCA had reared a couple a few years ago, but the young girl involved had left and there was nothing in reference books to go by. I decided to use goat's milk, the same as I would do for any small mammals. Using a tiny syringe, the babies took the food well and I lined the nestbox with tissue which was replaced every time I fed them. Unfortunately, the baby that the cat had caught died during the first night, but the others continued to feed well. Cats can do a lot of damage when catching anything as their needlesharp teeth pierce deep into the resulting wounds, causing infection which can often be fatal. Normally we would inject with antibiotics when faced with a cat wound, but these babies were so small that the injection alone would probably have been fatal, so we had let the baby take its chances.

I noticed that after a day or so, their droppings started to get loose and thought that maybe the milk was too rich for them. Obviously any milk would be different from what they had been having, and to change a diet in anything so small can cause all sorts of problems. Once diarrhoea sets in, babies lose fluids quickly and they dehydrate. After changing them to lectade, I could see that two were looking quite poorly. I rang Barry, the vet, and he wanted to see them immediately, so without further ado they were all taken in to the surgery. With infinite patience, he checked each tiny baby over and decided it was necessary to inject fluids into the two poorly ones. With great care, the fluids were put into the scruff of the neck, about the only place you could collect enough skin to hold. His concern for them was obvious, and without any reference works on this species to consult, he was only acting on instinct. It is at times like these when I appreciate the care he gives to creatures so small that others would merely dismiss them. I returned home with them, feeling a little bit more optimistic.

On adjusting their diet they began to improve, but while they had had the tummy upset their urine had been strong, and this had burnt the fur from their tails and between their legs and made them very sore. I felt so sorry for them as they waddled out of their nests, legs apart where it was so sore. Talking over the problem with Mandy, she said 'what a shame, and they are only babies'. I suddenly realized she was right. By the time the next feed came around, I was armed with nappy wipes, baby powder and zinc and castor oil cream. Each tiny bottom was wiped, powdered and smarmed in cream. Gradually the soreness disappeared and a week later, new fur could be seen coming through on their legs and tails. We had won the day! They were also becoming very agile and I learnt to be very quick when cleaning them out. Weaning them was not very easy, as it was a question of finding things to suit their diet. In the wild their tastes vary according to the season, and they are known to take pollen, flowers, fruits, insects and nuts. They love hazel nuts and eat them from the branches when they are still green. Eating from the side of the nut, they gnaw a complete circle to get into the kernel inside. Dropping the shell to the ground when they have finished leaves the tell-tale sign of dormouse occupation, and this is one sure way of telling that dormice are present when surveying areas.

All my five babies weaned successfully, and these, together with other young dormice taken from the wild under licence, which were too small to survive the winter, formed a group of animals to be used for captive breeding. This is part of the National Programme for Captive Breeding of the Common Dormouse, which will enable eventual release into areas where they have become extinct. This is all done under the umbrella of the licence which Doug holds for keeping the animals. Several of us have cages in specially designed buildings where we keep unrelated pairs or trios, and their youngsters will eventually be released in suitable areas where dormice have become extinct. I am very pleased to say that one of the little chaps that I reared fathered three offspring the following year.

A lot of voluntary work goes into the monitoring and surveying of areas of land, so that we can find out more about the animals that we live alongside. Indeed, such is the amount of labour and dedication given to this kind of work, by both Doug and Michael Woods, that in 1993 they were presented with medals from the Mammal Society to acknowledge the importance of all that they have done.

Ask any forester what they think of the grey squirrel and they will tell you that the 'tree rat' is a damned nuisance. In large numbers they may well be, but for the likes of you and me, they really are rather pretty. We have some large walnut trees in our orchard, and on occasions, grey squirrels have been seen scampering over the log pile, attracted to the area by the food supply.

Cyril was a cutie. He was found on the Somerset Levels by a lady out walking. Cold and shivering, he was lying on the ground so she brought him in to us. He was about three weeks old, and I must admit that he did look a bit like a rat as his tail was not bushy yet and his head looked rather large. He also had very large feet; when I placed him in a box by the Rayburn he covered his face with his large hands, digits spread out so that he could still peek through and take in what was happening. Curled in a ball, his long tail circled his body ending tidily between his ears. Quietly, I sorted out a feeding syringe and mixed up some milk; when all this was done, I moved towards the Rayburn to see how he was. Now that he was nice and warm, two little paws and a head peeped over the edge of the box with ears twitching, showing great interest in what I was doing. There was no need to lift him out. Recognizing the smell of milk, he climbed up my sleeve, chattering to make me understand just how hungry he was. On my offering him the syringe, he sat on his hind legs and cupped his paws around the tube, drinking heartily. If only they were all as easy as this! Maybe I look different, and I certainly was not the right colour, but he was quite prepared to accept me as Mum. Clambering over my jumper, once he had had his fill, he was fascinated with my hair and chattered contentedly next to my ear. It is at times like these that the thought of how they can bite flashes across your mind, but discovering the neckline of my sweater he slipped under the collar next to my shirt, curled up and promptly fell asleep.

As I have said before, one animal on its own is never a good thing, and I tried to spend as much time with him as I could for company. As luck would have it, a week later three other baby squirrels were picked up in Weston-super-Mare. A squirrel had been found dead outside a house in the morning, and by late afternoon, three baby squirrels were venturing out of a nest in a tree in the garden, hungrily calling for their mother who had not returned. We were pleased to have them brought in as there was hardly any age difference between them and Cyril. They took their food just as easily as Cyril, and I placed each one in with him as I fed them in turn. Having handled them, they smelt of me and the box was soon full of youngsters sniffing and greeting each other before eventually settling down to sleep in a ball of heads and tails. The box was accepted as the nest, and as they were still so young, they did not attempt to leave the box until I came with the milk. They soon recognized the sound of food being prepared, and four little faces with matching pairs of paws peered over the edge of the box waiting for dinner to be served. Similar to the dormice, they have very fine claws so that when they climbed on to me, it was difficult to get them off. They knew how far they could venture and still be safe, and I could take them outside to feed and know they would stay on me. Obviously, as they got older, the further they would go, until eventually it was time for them to go into an aviary. It is illegal to release grey squirrels once captured as they are classed as vermin. We put ours in an aviary for the first winter, but have always found that in the spring they manage to chew a hole in the wire and escape.

Sally is our latest squirrel. She was brought in by some visitors who had gone for a walk in the park; Sally must have lost her mum, and was so hungry that she was coming up to people and trying to suck their shoes. Surprisingly enough, she also has chewed a hole in her cage and is now making the most of her new-found freedom. Sally has learnt that there is a container of nuts in the reception, and if the visitors don't seem very helpful by way of supplying food, she goes and knocks on the window until someone comes out and gives her a nut. I can appreciate the damage squirrels can do, having had a garden rake chewed nearly in half when left briefly against the side of the house while I went for a cup of coffee – but I still think they look pretty!

The mink is not indigenous to this country, having been brought in from abroad for the fur industry. But when you consider that it takes 150 to make a full-length coat, it is good to hear that not so many are farmed for fur today. Now widespread in the British countryside, it was believed they would do considerable damage to native wildlife, particularly on the waterways, and they probably did when released by animal liberators in numbers of anything up to two or three hundred in one go in a single area. That kind of saturation in a territory, with each animal desperately trying to learn how to survive in the wild, would cause devastation amongst the animals they would prey upon. Now that the numbers have evened out, things have become more balanced. I think we must now accept them as part of our mammal population that does no more damage than any other predator in its own territory.

As mink are usually chocolate brown, we were surprised when sent a baby mink, found on some waste land, that was a beautiful silver-grey colour with a white bib. This colouring is called a mutation and is bred into some animals for colour variation in the fur industry, though it does also occasionally occur in the wild. Murphy, as we called him, was about three weeks old. Easy to rear, he was as playful as a young ferret and loved anything new, being full of inquisitiveness. We were doing a stand at a Summer Fête at a local school, and I decided to take Murphy along as I knew the children would enjoy seeing him. Derek was not sure it was such a good idea; he had never been keen on ferrets, and mink are very similar kinds of animals. 'If you take him, *you* will have to look after him', I was told. Sage came with us, and we took some baby tortoises, but Murphy stole the show with all his antics. Full of beans, I had him down my sweater, and he was wriggling up and down my sleeves, poking his head out of the cuffs, then at the neck, then down at the waist. The more the children laughed, the more he got excited and wriggled around. He was a great hit, but the last laugh was to be on me. I suddenly felt that warm and wet feeling that you instantly know as not being very pleasant. Murphy, having emptied both bladder and bowels between my shirt and sweater, was now tired after his games and ready to sleep. Placing him back in his box, and without a change of clothes, I did a clean-up job as best I could with a couple of tissues, but the entire mess had soaked right through my clothing; and anyone meeting me, not aware of what I had been doing, would certainly have thought my perfume left a great deal to be desired. I spent the rest of the time slightly more subdued, standing back from the tables so that people could not catch the odour that wafted around me, trying not to look at the expression on Derek's face which I can only describe as a smirk.

Murphy was one animal that we were unable to release, as being reared on his own he was far too tame. We made a special pen for him with a pond to swim in, and Doug sometimes took him out with him to lectures. Before one such occasion, when he had not taken him out for a while, we had noticed that Murphy was not so keen on being picked up, although he was still as friendly as ever. Doug asked if he could use him for a talk at a school and I said that he was welcome to, but that I was not sure that he was so easy to handle these days. 'He'll be all right,' said Doug, 'I'll collect him on my way through to the talk.'

Three sticking plasters later, the only thing that Doug had to show was the kind of bites one can get from a mink, rather than the animal itself! This therefore marked the end of Murphy's lecture days, but he still came up to the glass on his pen when people called him, and to see him roll and dive in the water was great fun. He died in his sleep in 1992 and was sorely missed by us all.

Whenever Sheena, my friend, comes to visit me, when the farm is open to the public, something always goes wrong to upset our plans. She was bringing a friend from the hotel where she worked and the idea was to have lunch out together and have a nice lazy day. Travelling down from Oxford, she expected to be arriving at the farm by about 11 a.m. A quick flick round the house to get it tidy, everywhere was staffed, I should be OK – or so I thought. With vacuum cleaner in hand, the first interruption of the day was a call from an elderly lady: she had an injured hedgehog in her garden and could I come and fetch it? Glancing at the clock, I said it would be no trouble at all, and did a quick mental calculation: half an hour there, half an hour back, which would still give me time to get the place clean before the guests arrive. You will have gathered, by these last-minute efforts, that we run on what is called 'crisis management' – which means that as there is so much to do, anything urgent is done straight away, and everything else gets left!

Grabbing the car keys, and carrying box and gloves, I called out to Derek as I crossed the yard, telling him where I was off to. He was busy cleaning out the pigs. 'What about Sheena?' he asked.

'Oh, I shall be back in time for her' I replied, and off I went.

Following the instructions, I found the pretty cottage very easily. Mrs Hayden answered the doorbell promptly. This was not going to take very long, I thought, but from there things went downhill. I mistakenly remarked on her lovely garden, to which she responded by telling me how much it had been the pride and joy of her husband, who had sadly just recently died. She did not see many people now and it was so nice to meet someone who liked gardening. She kindly showed me round, naming all the plants and telling me with fond memories how they had acquired certain shrubs, now fully established and flowering in their full glory. It was a haven for butterflies, insects and birds and I could remember thinking that, one day, I would love to have such a garden as this. Taking a quick look at my watch, and seeing how the time had gone by, I gently steered the conversation to the hedgehog – maybe we ought to have a look at it, did she have it in a box? 'Oh, no' was the reply; it was smelling and she had not liked the idea of picking it up. We would find it by the back of the house, near the hedge. Trying to hide my disappointment, I was not surprised to find that the hedgehog was no longer in the site where it was first seen, and the more she described its condition, the more I realized the urgency of finding it. Sheena won't mind if I am a little bit late, I thought, as I crawled along the hedgerow trying to find the elusive patient. I found it more by smell than by seeing it, as the stench of maggots pinpointed the place where the poor animal was resting. Picking it up quickly, I took it to the carrying case and, apologizing to Mrs Hayden that I could stay no longer, I made my departure with the promise to ring her and keep her informed of the hedgehog's progress.

Arriving back home just before 11 a.m. I was relieved to find that Sheena had not arrived yet. Calling to Mandy to come and help, I went upstairs to attend to the hedgehog. Stepping over the vacuum cleaner, which unfortunately had not moved while

I had been away, I cleared the kitchen table and Mandy came in armed with tweezers, fly powder and all the bits and pieces. I carefully lay the sickly hedgehog on an old towel; she was too ill to bother to roll up. Secondary fly strike covered her ears and eyes, but further advanced maggots were writhing in a wound by her back legs. Having assessed her condition, we set to work removing the maggots. Two people concentrating over this poor animal, with removed maggots crawling in a dish, and fleas deserting their host and hopping on a nice clean towel, was the sight that greeted Sheena and her friend Sue, as they came up to the kitchen on their arrival – not to mention the smell and the vacuum cleaner they tripped over. Apologizing, I suggested they might like to have coffee in the tearoom, and I would join them as soon as I could. Luckily Sheena has a good sense of humour (but not a strong stomach), and she backed away very quickly, saying it was no problem at all, and was gone.

By the time we had cleaned the hedgehog up, dusted her and placed her in the warm to overcome her trauma, some considerable time had elapsed. Sheena and Sue had finished their coffee and were sauntering around the farm looking at the animals. Catching up with them, I told them the story behind the hedgehog and we discussed our plans for lunch. I preferred to have lunch away from the farm, just to have a break, so said I would change and then we could drive to a local pub. I did not even make it back to the house before someone intercepted me with a cardboard box. It was a nest of starlings. Council workers were putting new roofs on the houses in the village (they had brought birds up to us before) and had come upon the nest as they removed the tiles. The mother would not return now they had disturbed the area, so they had brought them to us. Out of the corner of my eye, I could see that Sheena and Sue were now back in the yard and waiting for me to come out for lunch.

'No trouble at all,' I heard myself saying yet again, and I carried the starlings into the dairy, to put them under some heat. 'Shan't be long,' I called to Sheena, as they went by; 'Just got to get some food ready.' Mixing up the usual ingredients, I collared Mandy to see if she would mind feeding them while I was out for lunch, and that was all right. I checked on the hedgehog, who by now was looking a little bit better and had drunk some of the lectade water that had been given to her. Dashing upstairs to have a quick wash, and jumping over the vacuum cleaner (which still hadn't moved) I then sprinted to the bedroom to get some clean clothes on. The bedside clock told me it was 1.15 p.m. If I did not hurry, we would be too late to order any food. The telephone rang. Someone else can answer that, I thought, and continued to dress. One leg inside a clean pair of trousers and the telephone rang a single tone, meaning it was an internal call, and probably for me. Damn! I thought, struggling to pull on the trousers and reach the kitchen extension at the same time.

'Hello', I said breezily. (How do I manage to sound so cheerful sometimes?) It was Derek. He had just taken a call from a vet at Worle, who had had a roe deer fawn brought into them: could we take it on? He said that he would collect it, but would I be here to see to it when he got back? Mentally changing our lunch plans, I said yes, and went to get the equipment that Derek needed. Placing a hot water bottle in with a clean blanket in a carrying case for him, I made my way down to the office. Sheena and Sue sat patiently waiting, having returned to the yard yet again. Derek said his goodbyes, and left me to explain that lunch was going to have to be at the farm after all so that I could see to the fawn when it arrived. For Sue and Sheena, the thought of seeing a fawn made up for the change of plans, and at least we did manage to have lunch together in the tearoom.

Derek was back in no time at all and we were only just finishing lunch as he returned. Never having dealt with a roe fawn before, I was as inquisitive as the others and we took the carrying case upstairs to the privacy of our own quarters. The little fawn was only about five days old. Roe deer often leave their young sleeping in cover, returning to feed them at different times of the day, and often people come across them thinking they are lost when really the mother knows exactly where she has left her young.

This fawn was found tangled in the bramble bushes and calling in distress, and was taken to the local vet. We named him Bramble. I had never seen anything so beautiful and perfect in every way. He was 15 inches from the tip of his ears to his feet. His ears looked slightly large for the shape of his head and his finely boned face. White spots dappled his back and his long gangling legs looked too fine to carry his weight. Deer are incredibly nervous, and if you have to hand-rear the young, for once it is advocated that you keep them indoors so that they will get used to you, to your smell and noises. Being placed in a shed and approached to be fed on occasions would terrify them so much they would never feed;

but giving them the chance of getting used to you improves the situation, although they are still notoriously difficult to get to feed from a bottle and hand-rear. Bramble was very hungry, but even so it took some time and much trial and error before I found a teat that he would take to. Sheena and Sue, after seeing him, had left me to it so as not to frighten him more than was necessary. So once I had fed him and settled him back in his box. I left him in peace in the kitchen and went to find them. They were just getting ready to leave – another full day at Pauline's where they had seen all of half an hour of her. One day, Sheena, we will have more time!

Once the farm was closed for the day, I went upstairs to get tea ready. Feeding Bramble again, I placed him back in his carrying box, but this time left the door open. The family carried on with our tea and watching television, trying not to take too much notice of him. After an hour, he stood up and gracefully poked his head out of the box. Barney was very interested, but the deer did not seem to mind him at all and decided to climb out of the box. Shaking his body, he sniffed the floor and quietly explored the room, stopping to sniff our legs and discovering the dog's water bowl. He snorted the water out of his nostrils and, putting his head up, quivered his lips in distaste. After taking another feed later in the evening he did not return to his box, but settled out of sight behind the chair; that became his special place. I suppose, really, it was similar to hiding in the grass, out of sight, while he was on his own. By the next day, he had bonded to me, and my entrance to the room was greeted with a pipping noise. He had found his energy too, and day by day he became braver in the distance he would move around the house. They say that Walt Disney based Bambi on a roe deer fawn, and when Bramble would charge down the hall, and then put his brakes on, his legs would slide out sideways just as it is depicted in the cartoon.

I have always loved my badgers, but here was an animal who completely took me over. In the evenings we went out into the garden, once everyone had gone, and he would gambol and play, jumping sideways as he challenged the dogs. I hung dog rose and bramble branches in the kitchen for him to browse as he got a little older, and also a tray of earth, as they take earth from an early age. It must contain minerals that they need. I told the RSPCA that I had him, and Colin thought it best that I kept him to the age of five weeks, by which time he would be weaned; then I would have to make the break and let him go to the Wildlife Unit, to be put in a pen with other orphans to become wild and finally released. Every day, I could see that this was going to become increasingly difficult as I became more and more attached to him. Knowing that two-thirds of everything in the wild dies in its first year, I yearned to have a pen built for him and keep him on the farm, safe from all dangers he would find in the big world.

I decided to take him for a walk in the homeground as he followed me in the garden. As we approached the alleyways, he sensed the open space and sprinted away, ears back, feeling the rush of the wind on his face. With my heart in my mouth, I watched and hoped he would come back. At about twenty to thirty yards he found his safe distance and stopped, and turning, he charged back to me. Having walked badgers, which follow close to heel, this was a new experience, but I got used to the sight of his crashing through the grass, before finally coming back to my side. It was then, seeing his sheer pleasure at being able to run free, that I knew I could not keep him. Those walks are treasured memories, my mental pictures of him standing in the fields brilliant with buttercups in the sunshine, and quiet evenings in the garden.

All too soon he was weaned and it was time for him to go and join his own kind at the Wildlife Unit. Leaving him was one of the most difficult things I have ever done. Colin told me several weeks later that Bramble was almost as wild as the others, but would stand his ground just that little bit longer than the others, when the staff went into the large enclosure, before running away. Roe deer live all around the area of the Wildlife Unit and the staff just open the gates of the paddocks and the young deer go in their own time. I hope he made his first year, and I like to think of him as a proud stag with a group of his own females.

One thing I have learnt is that all my animals are just on loan and must eventually go back to where they belong. A saying I shall always remember is: 'If you love it, let it go. If it returns, it is yours. If it doesn't, then it never was.'

9

More Badger Tales

Talk about being spoilt! While other keen badger fanatics had to dress up warm and sit for hours in the dark in the hope of seeing a badger, here was I with three badgers in an observation sett, where I could watch them in a darkened room any time I wanted to. My three badgers, Willow, Bluebell and Primrose, had settled in their new home and, even during the day, there were times when they would be awake, playing or preening, giving a real insight into the behaviour that would normally go on underground in their setts. They love to scratch and preen: using their teeth they nibble through their coats, and scratch roughly at their hips with both their front paws, twisting themselves to reach as far as they can; then they will sit on their haunches like a fat bear and really claw through the front of their tummies and up to their chests. They would always sleep together, bodies completely entwined so that sometimes it was difficult to make out where one finished and another started! Occasionally, I would still share a walk with them but in the main I left them to their own independence.

Each morning, I would go down and unlock the doors to the observation room and check that all was well before starting the day's chores. One day at the end of January, only a few weeks after they had been given complete freedom, I went to look at them and could see that only Bluebell and Primrose were curled up together.

Willow was missing. Unlocking the door into the area where the chambers were, I called the badgers, hoping that he was down one of the tunnels. Primrose was the first to wake; poking her head out from the back entrance to the chambers, she lazily stretched her front legs and threw her head back with a long yawn. Bluebell barged past, inquisitive as to my presence at that time of day, and I sat by the side of the chambers. They both approached me, greeting me with the soft 'Uv-vuv-vuv-vuv' noise. Bluebell climbed on to my lap, and Primrose turned and scented my shoes and then sat waiting expectantly, as if they also thought that Willow would come out. But there was no other noise to be heard, and calling again, I knew that he wasn't there. Fussing them, I talked to them – even asked them if they knew where he was, but in my heart, I knew I was not going to see him again. First Primrose, then Bluebell returned to the chambers, fluffing up the straw bedding, and finally settling down to sleep again but not before looking again towards the tunnels, as if half expecting Willow to blunder in in his usual way. I made my way slowly back to the farmhouse, checking the road as I looked over the wall, in case he had met with an accident. On breaking the news to Derek and Mandy, they both said that perhaps he would be back the next night, and for the rest of the day we all kept a look-out for him, but he was not to be seen.

The next morning found both the girls curled up together but not Willow, and we have never seen or heard of him since. It was really the wrong time of year for him to have wandered off, and he must either have strayed too far and got lost or come to grief. We shall never know. Certainly local people, once they knew we had lost one of our badgers, either brought or reported all the dead badgers found in the local vicinity. (Poor Derek got quite fed up with digging holes!) All the ones that we saw were either the wrong sex or the wrong markings. Willow had always been such a character and I shall always have many memories of him – first as such a tiny bald little badger who could be so obstinate, and who eventually grew into a fine young male whose sense of fun and boisterousness had us all, including Barney the dog, nearly at the end of our tethers at times. It was the end of a very precious relationship. I dearly hope that he survived and found a territory of his own.

This left us with the two girls who, to start with, would still sleep with their heads turned towards the tunnels, as if waiting for him to return; but after a couple of weeks they gave up and no longer turned to look for him if we were out together. Bluebell and Primrose spent the rest of the winter all on their own.

It was late one evening in early March that I heard a frantic scratching at the front door. As I opened it, Bluebell trundled in. It was the first time she had been in the house since she was a cub. She climbed the stairs and scent-marked the carpet as she made her way around the kitchen, climbing up on the chairs as she explored the rooms. I left the door open so that she could leave when she wanted, and once she had done her tour, she made her way back down the stairs and out into the garden. The following evening she returned and again scratched to come in. 'You've started something now,' was the passing remark from Derek, as he lifted his feet on to the chair, so that Bluebell could not scent his feet. I could not really understand why, after all this time, she now wanted to come into the house.

Her next visit, the following evening, showed us the reason. She had a nasty bite wound on her back. Another badger must have been bothering them at the sett, and lost for what to do, she had come to us to do something about it. The period from January to May is the territorial time of year for badgers. It is the season when a lot of marking by dung pits is done to establish territories and warn other badgers away. This other badger was encroaching on to Bluebell's and Primrose's area and they were coming to blows. I decided to shut the badger gate and keep them both secure in the sett and enclosures. It meant that I had to visit them in the evenings, instead of meeting up in the yard, but they seemed much more settled and secure and got back to their silly habits of charging and playing. Even at four years of age, Bluebell would play quite roughly. It's a good job that I usually have a thick coat on as she will grab the sleeve and shake it like a dog, or grip my whole arm with all four feet and take my hand in her mouth, although without actually hurting me (not really, anyway!).

I opened the badger gate again in May and we had no further trouble. The farm opened for the summer season and Simon King officially opened the observation sett for us. Visitors thoroughly enjoyed being able to see the badgers, many people never having seen one alive before.

As the summer days got longer, I would go and spend some time with the girls in the enclosure before they started to go foraging, and I noticed marks on Primrose to show that she had been mating and was obviously meeting up with other badgers. There is a very large sett a couple of fields away. It has been there for over a hundred years but has only supported a small family group. When we once visited, we found a badger skull thrown out with the spoil from where the badgers had been excavating old tunnels. It is thought that badgers sometimes bury their dead underground in a chamber and block it off. Generations later, young badgers re-open these chambers to enlarge their living area, and the bones from the buried badger are brought out with the excavated soil. How true this is nobody really knows, but certainly badger bones are found at different times in such a way that it would suggest that this is probably what happened.

Working outside on the farm in the evenings, we often saw Bluebell around but Primrose had more interesting things to do! It was only a matter of weeks before she also failed to return home. I was quite convinced she had joined the nearby group and did not have the same fear for her safety as I did for Willow.

A few weeks later, my supposition was confirmed when a villager in West Huntspill told me she had seen a badger that did not take a lot of notice of people, foraging with another badger in a field by a road that runs adjacent to ours. She had stood her ground longer than the other badger, when people entered the field to watch them, before eventually running off to join her partner. She looked very well, according to them. The whole aim of the sett was to return the badgers to the wild and the choice was theirs, so there was no point in worrying about her. (If she had managed to find a man – good for her!)

The only problem this left was the fact that Bluebell was now on her own, a thing that no badger likes. It just seemed so sad to see her asleep on her own. She seemed to rely very much on my company and made a great fuss of greeting me, with that lovely purring sound, and scenting me when we met. Bluebell always did spend a lot of time around the yard but never actually came into the house.

I worried that she would wander off, just to try and find some company, and when, a month later, on checking the sett, I found a completely empty observation sett, I thought immediately that this was what had happened. Maybe I should have kept her shut into the sett and enclosure to stop her wandering off, but I so wanted her to have her freedom. When I told Derek the bad news, we both felt very depressed at having lost all our badgers. When Mandy turned up for work I went into the dairy where we do our feeding, to tell her that Bluebell had gone as well. Leaning against the cupboard, I discussed with her why Bluebell would have gone. But then my attention was suddenly caught by a black and white face peering down from the open staircase that led up to the cheese room. Madam's nosiness had obviously been her downfall! Bluebell must have decided to scale the stairs to find out what was up there, but faced with the staircase going down, her confidence had left her and she had had to stay there for the rest of the night. On hearing my voice, she had realized help was at hand. Chiding her for being so silly, I carried her down the stairs and put her on the ground. She charged out of the dairy and made straight towards the observation sett, obviously upset at being out in the daylight. By the time I reached the observation sett, she was already in and settling down to get some sleep. Overjoyed that we had not lost her after all, we celebrated with cream cakes at coffee time!

Bluebell decided to dig a sett, nearer to the house. She started to dig near the foxes' pen and excavated huge amounts of soil and bricks. Badgers have been known to turn over stones weighing nearly fifty pounds in order to get at peanuts that had been placed underneath. Having designed a nice new home nearer to our house, the next evening's work was to drag bedding from the haybarn to the new sett leaving a huge swathe of hay as a bedding trail that must have been at least 100 metres long. After each night's labour she still religiously returned to the observation sett and has, so far, never moved out. It was almost as if she was building an emergency home in case it was ever needed!

As the 1991 season was coming to an end, in September, a vet at Glastonbury contacted me. They had a young male badger, this year's cub, with bite wounds where he had obviously been evicted from his group. He had been knocked down by a car and had injured his leg. Now that he had been treated and was on the mend, they were not sure what to do with him as he was going to need a time of care before being released; even then, he had no real territory to return to. I offered to pick him up and decided to try and integrate him with Bluebell.

It was quite easy to find the vet's; and once I had overcome the problem of moving the badger from the vet's cage to the one I had brought with me, I was soon sitting in my car, quite happy with the thought of having a friend for Bluebell. The veterinary nurse waved goodbye, her face showing relief at getting rid of such a smelly, and not always very co-operative, patient. Badgers have the dentition of a carnivore and, with the weight and power that they have in their bodies, are capable of amputating fingers. It is not that they are fierce or vicious, but any animals, caught in a situation they do not understand, will retaliate in any way that they can. People who deal with badgers, therefore, either have fingers missing(!) or have learnt the art of handling them properly.

When you keep a badger in captivity, you must notify English Nature as they are a protected species and can only be held for welfare purposes without requiring a licence. Now that we have several through at different times, we keep a record which is sent in every so often; but in isolated cases, as was the situation at that time, the authorities must be notified. So having done this, my next move was to work out how and when to integrate this young badger in with Bluebell.

The sett had been designed so that it could be split into two sections, allowing nose contact only through wire doors. I shut off the third chamber and bolted the badger gate so that the chambers and enclosure was the only area available to them. The new badger was named Muffin. This name was given to him by the lady who found him in the road and took him to the vet.

I decided to place Muffin in his part of the sett in the morning, which is the time when badgers are more lethargic and I thought they would have some time before being completely aware of the other's existence. When I took the box into the enclosure, Bluebell came out to investigate. She sniffed around the box, her tail swishing angrily at the intruder, and the huffing noises she was making left the young male badger under no illusion that he was not wanted. Moving into the back of the box, he tried to make himself as small as possible. I opened the glass front of what was to be Muffin's chamber and tipped him in, quickly closing it again before the irate Bluebell could get in and show him how much she cared. It is at times like these that you get an uneasy feeling that maybe this is not such a good idea. Treating me with complete disdain, Bluebell ignored my attempts of fussing her and continued her noisy efforts and tail-swishing around the chamber, in the middle of which sat a trembling young badger in an alien world. After a few hours Muffin, through either normal tiredness or nervous exhaustion, curled up and went to sleep; Bluebell, having returned to her chamber, was not sleeping but staring at the tunnels, aware that her home had been invaded by a stranger.

After a couple of days, they had both got used to the other's presence, Muffin no longer frightened by Bluebell moving around. She still cursed him as she passed his chamber but the tail-swishing had stopped, and I had hopes that maybe things were improving.

Luckily, a cleaner called Leigh was in the viewing room by the sett on the evening when the accident happened: there was a terrific amount of blood-curdling screaming as Bluebell attacked Muffin. Leigh dashed to the house: grabbing my keys, I collected some blankets and raced back to the sett to sort them out. Hurriedly opening the chamber front of Bluebell's section of the sett and shouting at her, I managed to cover Muffin in the blanket and pull him out. I could feel Muffin's heart pounding away but he relaxed in the darkness of being covered up and I carried him back to the house to look at the damage. He had a nasty bite to his neck, definitely needing stitches and I immediately took him to Barry, our vet, for attention. I just could not understand how he had managed to get in with Bluebell. The tunnels had still been shut off and the wire doors all shut.

When we returned from the vet's, I left Muffin in the kitchen to sleep off his anaesthetic and went to investigate how the accident had occurred. Bluebell looked a little sheepish, and was now sniffing around Muffin's chamber, as if she could not make out where he had gone. A few strands of his hair, by the wire in the lighting box, gave the clue as to what had happened. Although the chambers are completely separated, there is a lighting box that runs over all three chambers. Muffin had climbed up into the lighting box, crawled along and probably descended on a sleeping Bluebell in the next chamber, who understandably retaliated at such an unexpected intrusion. Having blocked off the lighting box, I returned Muffin to his chamber and things settled back to the indifference that had reigned before.

After two weeks, I reluctantly removed the wire doors and waited to see what would happen. Nothing. They would have nothing to do with each other; a very lonely Bluebell slept in one chamber and a small, shy Muffin scraped the straw round him before settling to sleep in another chamber on his own. I wished I had never started it. Here was Bluebell, with a young intruder she obviously did not like in her sett, and a confused youngster feeling totally rejected.

It was five depressing weeks before I went in one Saturday morning and my heart skipped a beat. There, snuggled together for the first time, were Muffin and Bluebell. They had finally accepted each other. Muffin was on his back, his front paws twitching as he slept with Bluebell's body curved against him and her head resting on his stomach. At last, all the worrying had been worth it.

In the meantime, as a member of the Somerset Trust Badger Group, I was becoming more involved in their activities. Members are involved in many kinds of ways, some helping with badger problems in gardens or on farms, others doing surveys or even fund-raising, but I had offered to help with road casualties and injured badgers. Not wishing for other wild badgers to be near our own sett, we had a special holding pen built with a heat lamp which was very quickly in use. Badgers come in to us for mainly two reasons. Firstly, because a badger is territorial, much fighting goes on within the species. A badger can survive quite horrific injuries and to a certain extent will accept it all as part of life, but sometimes these bites become infected making the animal seriously ill; and with the secondary problem of fly strike, which soon turns to maggots, the ailing animal will eventually die a slow death unless chanced upon by a person prepared to take some action.

You will be surprised just how many people will not want to get involved. I had a badger brought in to me by a friend, Kate, who, despite an appointment that she had to keep, found the time to collect this injured animal from the field it had lain in for three days, and brought it to us for attention – this involved a round trip of at least 50 miles. She had only heard of its plight through a conversation in a pub where a gentleman remarked that he had passed the badger each day as he walked his dog, lying in the same spot, and was surprised that it had neither moved nor died. That sow badger had serious back injuries and had to be put to sleep, but how much better to have ended her days quietly than to have allowed her to suffer. She had been in very good condition weight-wise, and to have had to wait for death to come through dehydration and hunger would have taken several weeks. All she needed was a compassionate person prepared to take some action, even if it had only been a telephone call to a local badger group or the RSPCA.

Road casualties are the second main cause for our work. Over 45,000 badgers are killed on our roads each year and when you consider that there are an estimated 54,000 family groups throughout the country, you are talking about, on average, one member of every social group being killed on the roads each year.

Many casualties that we get called to are often thought to be dead. Even our own vet, to his own shame, passed a badger on the side of the road which he was sure was dead, only to be called back to it an hour later, by someone who had discovered it was still alive. Barry has now done quite a lot of work with badgers that were road casualties, and has a very good success rate with them now that, as a general procedure, he gives them an intravenous drip of glucose saline.

Derek and I responded to a call late one night: a gentleman and his wife were returning from visiting their friends that evening in their car and had found a badger knocked down at the side of the road. We asked him to cover it with a blanket, and he offered to wait by the badger until we arrived to make sure that we found it. She was barely breathing, and showing muscle spasms of an animal very close to death. Quickly putting her into a cage, we took the man's telephone number and promised to let him know the outcome the following day. On reaching home, I rang through to Barry, apologizing for the late hour of calling. We arranged to meet at the surgery in fifteen minutes although I wondered if it was going to be too late. By the time I reached the surgery, Barry had already arrived and was switching on the lights. Lifting her carefully on to the table, Barry examined her, soothing her as he moved her around and then, having prepared her, connected an intravenous drip. I was the one who was going to return home for a coffee, but he would stay and monitor her for at least another hour before he could consider leaving her. Dedication has to come from all those involved.

I collected her late the next day and put her into our care pen. She was suffering from severe concussion, and to start with all I could do was to syringe fluids into her mouth at regular intervals. Slowly she recovered consciousness but made no attempt to move. I decided to try her with solids. Taking some food in my hand, I offered it to her. Sensing that I meant no harm, she gently took each piece, mouthing so carefully, as if she wanted to make sure that she did not catch my hand.

The couple that had found her visited her over the weekend and were thrilled that she was still alive, although I was careful to make sure that they understood there could still be complications. They had never seen a live badger before and took great interest in her recovery.

A week later saw a badger who was ready to go home. Eating

well, she had put on weight and luckily had no other injuries so was completely agile. We always release at night, the time that badgers would naturally be out. The later the better, to avoid the extra problem of traffic. I arranged to meet the couple at the same spot as she was found, to see her finally released. It is never so easy to get badgers, once healthy, back into a carrying box, as it is when you pick them up injured! Still, we managed, and arrived at the given time to meet them.

George Pearce, who does a lot of work with badgers and has advised me on several occasions, will tell you that when you release a badger, it will always turn and say thank you before it goes. He is usually right; certainly in this case, it was so. Standing the carrier on the ground, we opened the front and stood back to allow the badger to take its time in coming out. There was enough light that night to watch without using a torch. The badger came out of the box and sniffed the air. Turning immediately to her left, she knew where she was going and she started to make her way down a path, but briefly she turned, held up a paw, glanced at us, sniffed the air and was gone. That is enough thanks for anyone.

Not every call turns out to be what you think it is – and I hope that from this tale my husband's infinite patience will shine through!

As it is very busy during the season, it is not always easy to find the time to cook proper meals each evening, but I make a point on Sundays to make an effort and cook a roast meal. This is therefore the highlight of the week, as far as Derek is concerned. On this particular day the joint of lamb was roasting gently in the oven and I was busy preparing the vegetables. Another hour and we would all be sitting down having our evening meal.

It was half past six and Derek was busy shutting up the Visitor Centre having just said goodbye to the last of the day's visitors. The telephone rang and he answered it. Buzzing me upstairs, he cheerfully said. 'It's a call for you, and I've nearly finished so I'll be up soon.' Placing the receiver down, the call was redirected to me. It was Doug. The RSPCA at Exeter had received a call concerning a dead badger and had contacted Doug Woods, as chairman of the Somerset Trust Badger Group, to action the call.

'Sorry to trouble you, mate, on a Sunday, but I've had a call concerning a dead badger on the side of the road, with a couple of cubs running around. I'm a bit tied up, and wondered if you could go – any chance?'

I looked at the saucepans simmering on the stove, made a mental note to be nice to Derek, and said that yes, I would go. The badger was about half an hour's journey from us, and quite difficult to find, so the person who had reported it had said that if we called at his house, he would take us to where the dead badger was.

I switched all the rings and the oven off, left a note for the boys to say dinner would be late, and went to break the news to Derek. Ten minutes later, our car was making its way towards Bishop's Lydeard. We had a carrying case in the back, catching equipment, food for the badgers and map. Derek sat tight-lipped, driving, and I was trying to appreciate the early summer blossom that bedecked the hedgerow. It was a lovely summer's evening but there was a definite cold wind blowing in the car. By the time we reached the village, Derek had mellowed and had even agreed that it was a pleasant drive despite the fact that his tummy was rumbling. Following the instructions to find the house, we turned into a new housing estate, and finding the right close, pulled up outside the house. The young man had been looking out for us as he came immediately out of the door and over to the car. 'If you follow me in your car, I will take you there. I'll pull in just before the dead badger as the road is very narrow', he said.

'Fine,' I replied and smiled.

'Can't be long', said the young man, 'my wife's got the dinner nearly ready'; and with that he made for his car.

'Lucky you' murmured Derek, starting the car, and we followed him down nearly two miles of twisting lanes. Pulling in at a passing place, the young man parked his car and we stopped behind him. I could see the dead badger in the road just ahead. As we made our way up to the body, three rabbits scampered out from the long grass in the verge and disappeared through the hedge. 'Oh,' said the young man, 'I wonder if it was rabbits that I saw and not badger cubs. We didn't stop the car when we passed and I only caught a glance at them.'

I did not dare to look at Derek. 'Never mind,' was my reply. 'At least if we look at the badger we shall be able to tell if it is a lactating female.'

As we made our way up to the dead badger, I explained about some of the work that the badger group does. Lifting the leg of the dead badger to see its sex, I dropped it again and turned to the young man. 'No need to worry, the badger is not a lactating female, so even if you did see some cubs, their mother is still hopefully alive.' I thanked him for his time and he quickly made his departure to get back to his dinner.

Derek climbed up the bank to throw the body into the hedge, to allow nature to take its course, and I passed the badger up to him. Glancing at it, he looked at me and laughed; 'No wonder it isn't lactating', he said, 'it's a ****** boar!' The family sat down to Sunday dinner at 10.30 that evening, and it's not quite the same by that time – but at least it was fun making up to Derek that night for making his dinner late!

I must say that all badger group members would far rather be called out to potential problems, even if they turn out to be not quite as expected, than ever to risk the possibility of a badger suffering because members of the public did not like to bother anyone.

Bluebell and Muffin spent a lot of time together now, and I opened the badger gate to allow them their freedom. Muffin had by now grown into a fine looking male; his head was broad and he was thick-set and muscular, a contrast to the scruffy, gaunt yearling he had been when he first arrived. Bluebell would still saunter up to see us, but if Muffin was caught unawares, he would scamper back to the sett. I decided to shut the badger gate again the following January to stop any problems happening as before, and it was during this period of containment that a badger called Wendy was brought to me. She came from the Yeovil area and had lost her territory. As the gates were shut on the sett, I tried to integrate her in with Bluebell and Muffin. Again there was a great deal of indifference but no real objection to her being there. In the three months that she was contained with them, I felt there was something not quite right about her. She moved around the chambers and enclosure and fed perfectly well but lived independently of the others.

May came round again and it was time to open the badger gate out into the fields. Wendy had been in the sett long enough to have made it her home, but still she did not interact with the others. Three days after the gate was opened, Wendy disappeared. She did not return the next day either, but the following morning we received a call from a lady living in a village three miles away. Wendy was in her garden, curled up in a ball but having made no attempt to hide in any way.

We picked her up and brought her home. I rang Colin at the RSPCA Wildlife Unit as I was sure now that there was some slight brain damage and I felt she could never be released. There was no point in my keeping her, as I could not keep her in and give the others their freedom. Colin was prepared to take her on and sort something out for her, so we took Wendy down to the Unit.

Whether it was the intrusion of Wendy in the sett, or just the fact that Muffin was now reaching maturity and needed to wander, but two weeks later Muffin also disappeared. Bluebell was once again on her own, although this time she did not seem so bothered as when the others had gone.

It was during this time that TB reared its ugly head on the farm. Although the milking herd had been sold in 1987, Derek kept just a few cows and does a daily milking demonstration for the visitors, explaining the different breeds and the change from hand to machine milking. As well as breeds such as Friesian, Jersey, Guernsey and Dexter, we had two beautiful Highland cows whose shaggy coats and huge horns were very impressive. Each farmer has to have all cattle tested for TB; usually, your own vet will come, inject a small amount of the vaccine into the neck of the animal and then return three days later to check and see if there has been any swelling. TB, although not eradicated, is very rarely found these days and one takes these tests as a matter of course. We were shocked when our Guernsey cow reacted, and after a re-test so did both the Highland cows. All three had to be sent for immediate slaughter.

The sight of those majestic animals walking onto the cattle lorry to be taken away was heartbreaking. We learn to accept on a farm that animals have to go to the market, and ones that become ill do at times have to be destroyed, but here were three healthy-looking animals that we had no choice in sending on. What was even more distressing was that when the carcases were examined and cultures grown, they were shown to have been false positives. This means that they were not carrying TB but had merely reacted to the test. However, we do appreciate that testing is necessary, as no one would like to see the disease as rampant as it was in the 1940s. By slaughtering cows that had TB which in the 1940s was as many as 40 per cent of some herds, it has meant that the proportion of infected cattle has now been reduced to around 0.04 per cent.

The Ministry has a policy that where TB is found on farms, the badger population on that farm is destroyed with the farmer's permission. Originally they were gassed; they are now cage-trapped and shot. The argument was that, as it is impossible to test live badgers, it was essential to kill the animals first and then test the carcases. This means that many uninfected badgers are killed.

There is another side to this, because in trapping the animals, others from the social group may escape and disperse into neighbouring badger territories. Should these animals be carriers themselves then there is the likelihood, especially through bites from fighting, of the disease being spread. Alternatively, once a badger population which could well have been healthy has been killed, the void area will attract other badgers, who in turn could be infected themselves. Many badger group members, including myself, are horrified at the slaughter of badgers in this way; also, as a farmer's wife I can share the grief of losing cows that you have reared from a calf and have known intimately, believing that each animal is as important as any other. I have heard it said that it costs the Ministry approximately £3,000 for every infected badger that is slaughtered in TB problem areas (in red tape, man-hours and equipment), not taking into account money paid out to the farmer in compensation for slaughtered cows.

Deer and other wild animals can also carry the disease but not enough research has been done into this. It has all been laid at the door of the badger. And yet the slaughter has not proved successful in reducing the occurrence of TB: cows can contract the disease from a badger or another cow, as well as from a human being and vice versa. The government is still deciding whether to bring in blood testing, but even this will not show up animals that have the bacteria dormant in the body, so they would be releasing potential carriers. The Ministry of Agriculture in Ireland have for a couple of years tried to solve this problem by feeding a dead oral vaccine which is put into pellets (and even coated in chocolate!) that are then mixed with peanuts and fed to the badgers. This does not interfere with the testing of the cattle and it is hoped that it will stop TB in badgers. No official reports have been published but the results so far look promising.

It is a very difficult and complex subject, but surely one thing is clear: that money should be put into research into finding a cure or, at the very least, a way of diagnosing the animal concerned so that neither healthy cattle nor badgers are killed through unreliable testing methods.

Dealing with several badgers through that summer, we were again presented with a young male with no territory to be returned to. Teasel was a road casualty that was picked up by some holidaymakers on their way home. Having found a local vet, they dropped him off for medical attention and carried on their journey home. No one thought to ask their names, nor where the badger had been found. I integrated him with Bluebell in the same way as I had with Muffin, and after the usual huffing and bad manners, I allowed them together. He was only a yearling and still had plenty of growing to do, but was very shy and quick to respond to unusual noises. This time Bluebell took to him quite quickly and they were soon curled up together. (I think she was becoming quite a floozie!) They seemed very happy together and, although I had no contact with Teasel, he got quite used to me opening the door; Bluebell would leave him to come and see me and then, when she had had enough fuss, she would return to him in the chamber. Eventually he did not even bother to lift his head.

We had wondered if Bluebell would ever have cubs, especially as she had the freedom to go outside and had had male badgers in with her. I had read that sometimes it is better if you do not disturb them too much during the winter months, so in the winter of 1991, I did not go in to see her quite so often.

We had some friends call in to see us, just at the beginning of January. Bob and Jenny had called in with their children to see the animals. 'Any chance of seeing the badgers?' Jenny asked hopefully. She remembered seeing them when we had them as cubs.

'As long as we do not make too much noise,' I replied, and the children were told to be as quiet as mice.

Opening the door to the sett, we all stood by the glass. Bluebell was asleep in a chamber on her own and Teasel had commandeered the largest chamber so he could stretch right out; he was lying on his back fast asleep, but the sudden noise of us entering woke him up and, frightened by the unexpected movement, he slipped into the tunnels at the back. I unlocked the door to the sett and called Bluebell to see if she would come out and meet us, but surprisingly enough, she remained sound asleep. Slightly worried, as I was not monitoring them very regularly, I went to the chamber and opened the lid. She did not move. Putting my hand in, she did not feel very warm and I got the impression of something that had died but was being kept warm by the straw around the body. With eager faces watching from the other side of the glass, I told them that she was so sound asleep, it was a shame to wake her, and they must wait for another day to see her properly. Closing the chamber up, I came out and took them back to the house for a cup of tea, not voicing my terrible inner thoughts.

Luckily, by that time our visitors had been with us for most of the afternoon, and they left soon after their drinks to make their way home. Derek and I immediately went down to the sett. Teasel was still in the tunnels, and we both went in and opened the chamber. I was so convinced Bluebell was dead that I reached in to pick her up. It was only then that she arched her body and raised her head to look at me, but did not seem to recognize me. I gently lowered her back into the chamber and covered her back over with the straw.

I went back to the house and got straight on the telephone to Doug Woods to ask his advice. He explained that although badgers do not hibernate, they do sleep very deeply and sometimes do not emerge from their sett for days, or even weeks if the weather is bad. Bluebell was either really sound asleep, or seriously ill, it was difficult to tell. To take her out whilst asleep would disturb her, but on the other hand there was the possibility she might need medical attention. She was in good condition and up until then had been eating well, so I decided to leave her alone and let nature take its course. The next day she was still asleep, but on checking her the following evening, she was wide awake and full of beans.

Badgers have delayed implantation. This means that although they can mate at any time of the year, the embryo is retained in the body without growing. It is thought that there are not enough hormones produced by the body for the embryos to implant, and as the badger starts to put on weight, ready for the winter, the hormones are stored in the fat. When the sow badgers become dormant in the winter months, their bodies start to live off the fat and a greater amount of hormones are released into the circulation. This causes the embryos to implant and start to grow and therefore, no matter when the sows were mated, nearly all the cubs are born in January or February.

I can remember having Bluebell out with me one evening late in February and telling her that I did not think she was going to have cubs, she was just plain fat. But the next day she proved me wrong. It was Derek who went in the next day and discovered Bluebell just cleaning up and settling down with two cubs. Rushing up to tell me, he found me in Reception with Jean and Edna, the two office staff. We all went to have a look. By now Bluebell had finished cleaning up and she had fluffed the straw up into a circular bed. With her head tucked between her front paws, she had drawn the cubs into the protection of her curved body. It was a picture of contentment, a dream come true for us, that we would be able to share her time rearing her first family. The soft chamber lights picked up the wriggling cubs as they searched for her teats, whickering in the urgency to find food. Soon they had successfully latched on to her, and their tiny pink tongues worked hard as they paddled softly with their paws against her belly to stimulate the milk to flow. The cubs were very small, only about four inches long, and were pink with no other markings at all. We were so thrilled.

I immediately rang Doug to let him know. It was seven weeks and two days from the time that we had found Bluebell torpid. When Jean went out to do the banking that morning, she brought back a bottle of wine for us to celebrate and a congratulations card for giving birth to a pair of twins for Bluebell, which we stuck on the glass in front of the chamber!

People so rarely get the chance to see badger cubs; as they are born underground, it is only when discovered accidentally that they would ever be seen. Here we had a chance of so easily watching the cubs grow, as long as we did not disturb Bluebell. I had not cleaned the glass on the chambers recently and it was difficult to see all that clearly, but I decided to wait a couple of days before going in. I had no idea how Bluebell was going to react. With glass cleaner and dusters in hand, I went into the back area, and began to think just how silly this was with nothing to protect me. Bluebell immediately came out of the chamber; the cubs that had been suckling were cast aside as she moved, and whickered their disapproval. She came straight to my feet, turned and scented my shoes – with relief, I realized she was going to be all right. I made no attempt to go close to the cubs or open the chamber; I just cleaned the glass and then went out. It was as if we had mutually agreed an unspoken arrangement, that as long as I left them alone, I could carry on as usual. Returning to the chamber, Bluebell turned all the bedding and cubs upside down, sorted it all out and settled down, gently pulling the cubs closely in towards her with those strong powerful claws that were now being used so delicately. The cubs, which by now were nearly three days old, had the faint stripe showing on the head and short fine hairs were just starting to come through. As they settled into the curve of their mother's body, the whickering stopped. Completely blind and deaf, they were totally reliant on Bluebell for their protection. You read in books that it is thought that the mother will sleep separately from the cubs, in a different chamber, but Bluebell slept with her cubs continuously; even when the cubs were eight months old, they all piled into one chamber together.

Each day the cubs grew stronger, but they mature very slowly. They seemed to respond to sound at the age of four weeks; their eyes opened at five weeks, and they were beginning to look like real little badgers. We were able to see when they started to take their first steps and when they began to play, rolling over like puppies and bumping into the tree roots as they got carried away with excitement. Occasionally, as they are more active during the day when tiny, you would see poor Bluebell trying to sleep with two cubs chewing her ears and clawing at her body in an attempt to get some response to their wish to play. But once Bluebell is sound asleep, you can forget it; and it would usually end up with the cubs giving up and just falling asleep draped across her body, with her completely oblivious underneath. There was only one time when Bluebell came out to see me and a cub came out as well. Excited at being in a new-found area, it scampered around like a bumble bee, whickering in glee, and passed over my feet completely unaware of my being there. I did not try to touch it and was not sure what Bluebell's reaction would be, but she led it back to the sett and that was the only time that one came out. For the rest of the time I had no contact with them at all, and despite going in and cleaning the glass, and daily putting food down for them, they remained totally wild. This is the best way, if they were to survive in the wild. I knew that one of the cubs was a male, but never having seen the two with bottoms up, I was still not sure of both their genders. We therefore gave them neutral names, Bracken and Fern.

By this time, for my sins, I had become the secretary of the Somerset Trust Badger Group and we had arranged a committee meeting at the farm. When Doug arrived, he said that Pat Turner, another committee member, had gone out to a badger problem and was hoping to arrive later. A sow had been run over near a house, and it had just been realized, three days later, that she had had two cubs, which were now hungry and crying. They were hoping to catch the cubs if they came above ground but they were clearly becoming weaker all the time. The meeting commenced.

Pat arrived, having driven hurriedly to the farm, with Kathy, another group member, cuddling just one cub (despite the fleas) which was very dehydrated and crying pitifully. Unfortunately, they had only managed to catch the one cub; the people living in the house had promised to look out for the other, but he was never found and must have died underground. I injected fluids under the skin of the cub, which was a little boy, wrapped him in a clean blanket with a hot water bottle, and rang the vet. It was Colin who was on duty, and as usual, we arranged to meet at the surgery. The committee meeting was forgotten about, as far as I was concerned, and I left them to get on with it. The cub cried all the way to the surgery. When Colin examined him, he agreed that he needed to be put on a drip and I left the cub in his care.

By the time I drove in to pick him up the next day, he was looking much better – still pathetically thin, but his eyes were brighter and he was certainly more lively. His coat seemed to stick out and so he was christened Thistle. He was a couple of weeks older than Bluebell's cubs, but then hers were born on 28 February so they were late cubs. I should think he was about eight weeks old and although he was feeding well he was too old to bond with me, so I would not be able to walk him, as I had my other cubs. Even so he was great fun, but the element of fear of sudden noises or movement was inborn from being reared in the wild. He was full of life and ready to do badgery things, and I have a hole (luckily, only a small one) in the carpet of our kitchen floor to prove it, where he dug through the floorboards one night. The next morning, during breakfast, I found that if I sat with my foot over the hole, Derek did not notice it. I went out and bought a mat.

Maybe it was time Thistle went out in a pen, but I did not like the thought of him being on his own. He was now looking much better; he was a typical roly-poly badger cub but his hair still gave him a spiky appearance. As luck would have it, Sue Boyes Kourkis from the Wiltshire Badger Group got in touch with me. They had a female badger cub who had been a road casualty, but although she was now healthy, she did not seem to be behaving normally. She did not play, or preen or even whicker. We wondered whether, if she was put with Thistle, it might help her interact. Sue and Mike, her husband, brought her down the next day. Thistle was moved out of the house (much to the relief of Derek) into a pen with Millie. She was slightly smaller than Thistle and had a slimmer figure but a very pretty face, with the fine-boned head of a sow badger. They took to each other immediately and Sue had the pleasure of seeing them curled up together before she left to go home. My idea was eventually to put them into the sett with Bluebell and her family, but quite how, I had not worked out yet. I had not completely made up my mind as the last thing I wanted to do was to upset Bluebell with her cubs.

I spent quite a few evenings watching through the wire to see how Millie and Thistle were getting on. Badgers that fight each other will still sometimes sleep in the same chamber, so it is important to watch the behaviour once they are awake. To start with Millie did not take a lot of notice of Thistle's attempts to get her to play. Lying on his side, he would dig gently at her with his front paws and mouth over her head. All she would do was poke her nose further between her front paws and whine in annoyance. If there was one thing that Thistle had it was determination, and it was not many nights later that I had the pleasure of watching them first preen each other and then scamper around like puppies, barging at each other and tumbling over together in a badger ball. Badgers must have company. For this reason, when I next visited Colin at the Wildlife Unit with some young barn owls, he gave me a young male cub to put with my orphan cubs. At the Wildlife Unit, they form family groups with badgers that have no territory and then eventually release them in monitored areas. Their recent family had just been moved out and this was an odd cub that had just come in, and Colin had nothing for it to go with. William was about two to three weeks younger than the others, and so slightly smaller, but what he lacked in size he made up for in boldness; and a spitting, growling cub was tipped into the pen with Thistle and Millie. They soon curled up together and later in the evening he was quick to join in the games.

All this time, Bluebell had kept Teasel away from the cubs and he had had to sleep in another section of the sett. In the wild the boar is kept out of the sett while the female has cubs, and so the males tend to wander at this time of year, which is why so many are often seen dead on the roads around springtime. I was on my way down to the badgers one evening, and I heard a terrible rumpus coming from the enclosure. Quickly making my way there, I could just see in the dim light that Teasel had one of the cubs in his mouth and was shaking it. The cubs by now were nearly ten weeks of age and were making full use of the sett and enclosure. From eight weeks onwards, cubs would usually start to emerge from their setts and start to explore, but not without their mother to protect them. Bluebell seemed oblivious of what was going on, and when I shouted at Teasel to make him drop the cub she realized I was there, and plodded over to see if I had any food. Cubs sometimes disappear from setts that are monitored and it would seem that sometimes the males attack them.

I talked the problem over with several people and was given various reasons for the disagreement between boar and cubs. At ten weeks after giving birth, it was likely that Bluebell would be coming into season, and the cubs could have been getting in the way of the male wishing to mate. Another suggestion was that because Teasel was a young male, he would not have the same patience as an older boar and might be just proving his superiority, or it could just be that he had a nasty nature and would attack young cubs anyway. One thing was clear: that left in the sett with them, Teasel would kill the cubs.

The situation was brought to a head one Saturday evening, when I went down to shut the access to the viewing room at the end of a busy day. Looking into the chambers, I could see that one of the cubs had a nasty bite on the neck that was going to need stitches. It had only just happened and the blood was oozing on to the straw bedding. Somehow, I was going to have to get out the cub, which had never before had any contact with me, and without Bluebell stopping me. My first move was to ring the vet to make sure someone could be there to stitch the cub up. Nicky, the lady vet, was on duty, and she very kindly said she would wait for me to bring the cub in. I asked Simon to help me because, as usual when these things happen it was Saturday, and where is Derek? Cricket!

The first thing I had to do was to anaesthetize Bluebell – not a very easy thing to do because, although I handled her and played with her, I had never tried to restrict her, and I knew I would only get one chance because if I upset her and she ran away, it was going to be an even more difficult situation. Simon waited outside with the injection and I got her out into the room. Scruffing her by the neck, I called Simon who came in and held her down as I injected. We both withdrew to give it time to work. Five minutes later, she was sleepy enough for us to pass her and board up the chambers to get the cub out, with a great deal of disapproval. Typically, we managed to catch the uninjured one first. Thick gloves were certainly the order of the day. I was fully aware of how angry Bluebell would be at what we were doing, if she came round before we finished. Pushing the cub into the carrying box, we withdrew all the boards and shut the sett back up, hoping Bluebell would not miss the cub before we got back. We weighed the cub and anaesthetized it so that Nicky could get on and stitch it as soon as we got there. The cub was still voicing its disapproval and fear as I started the journey to the vet. It suddenly went quiet, and I spent the rest of the journey mentally calculating whether I had given the right dose of anaesthetic, and hoping it was still alive!

Nicky set to work, the only comment being 'God, look at the fleas!'

She worked quickly, and I was soon returning home, still not sure what to do next. Placing the cub back in the alleyway, I went inside the observation room to see if Bluebell was all right. She was no longer in there but was out in the enclosure. My heart sank when I saw that the other cub had now been bitten and was shaking in fear in one of the chambers. Before Bluebell had time to return, I pulled the other cub out just by using a blanket that had been left behind. Speed rather than safety was the order of the day. Taking the other cub up to the sick room, I could see that the injuries were not quite so serious but it was going to need cleaning up and the cub would need an antibiotic injection. Simon, by this time, was out and the house was empty, so I decided to block off the boar badger from the sett, then clean up the cub and restrict Bluebell and the cubs just to the chambers until the next day when we would have to pull out the boar.

By the time I had blocked off the enclosure I was losing the light, so I went to shut the poultry houses up before seeing to the cub. All the bantams were secure, and I made my way into the orchard to shut up the geese and the larger poultry. This was the evening I was to catch Tripod in the act (the three-legged fox that escaped that spring). She was dragging the Brahma cockerel by its neck down the path. On seeing me, she opted for escape rather than food and ran off, leaving the bird stretched out on the grass. Picking up the poor fellow, who was still alive (just), I shut the geese and Brahma house up. I returned to the sick room, and carefully placed the bird in a heated pen; there was not much more that I could do for him. It was the muscles in his neck that were injured. He did recover eventually and lived to a ripe old age. The cub was next. By wrapping him totally in a blanket and just opening it where the injuries were, I was able to get him cleaned up. I now knew, having handled both the cubs, that they were both male. Returning him to the sett, there was no more I could do down there until the morning.

On Saturdays Derek has the day off, and I have to shut up at the end of the day, clean the shop floor and see to the bantams and poultry. Then on Sunday it's my day off and his turn to see to everything. I would rather get all the jobs done first and then sit to eat my meal at the end of the day no matter what time it is. With all the complications, I was still washing the shop floor at 11.30 p.m. when Derek rolled home. Cricket evidently continues after dark, and it is always necessary to analyse the complete game – usually at a nearby public house, for the want of anywhere better to go. 'I'll go and make you a nice cup of coffee', he said, guilty at the fact that I was still working.

When I had finished the floor and eventually made it upstairs, my coffee, now cold, was sitting on the middle of the kitchen table, and a trail of clothes was evidence that Derek had gone to bed! Making a fresh cup of coffee, I put some food together and was about to relax over my meal but I suddenly could not remember if I had shut one of the poultry houses in the orchard. Pulling my coat on yet again, I went out with torch in hand to check – you don't get a second chance with the foxes about. It was quite a bright night as I walked past the apple trees, and yes, I had shut the house up so all was well. I had just turned to go back to my meal when I heard a noise.

'Baaah, baaah' – but it wasn't coming from the orchard where the sheep were, it was coming from the homeground. Walking out to investigate, I found a lamb that had slipped into the ditch and struggled out but was now in the wrong field, and its plaintive cries were because it could not find its way back to the others. Opening the large gate between the two fields, I tried to manoeuvre the animal so that it would see the opened gate, but each time I chased round, as soon as it got near the gate, its blasted mother would call and it ran straight back along the hedge. With a mental picture of Derek curled up in bed and getting crosser by the minute, I decided I would do one more circuit before hauling Derek out to help. This time the lamb successfully found the gate and ran through bleating, its mother running up to meet it. Relieved, I returned to the house and sat and ate my meal at just past one in the morning. As I slipped quietly into bed a few minutes later Derek stirred, just long enough to say 'You're late coming to bed', and rolled over to snore gently but just loud enough to make getting to sleep difficult. How I stopped putting that pillow over his face, I'll never know.

The next day we did a complete change around. We took Teasel out of the sett, split the chambers and put Thistle, Millie and William in the sectioned-off area of the observation sett. Teasel was then housed in the care pen where the three cubs had been. Bluebell showed a lot of interest in the cubs but no disapproval. Teasel was allowed to get used to the care pen for a fortnight, and then we left the door open so that he could return if he wanted to. He did the first night but after that he was gone. At least he could still have nose contact with Bluebell through the wire and he knew the layout of the farm, and also there was the ready-made sett that Bluebell had dug near the house. So he had plenty of places to go to. We put food down for him each night by the enclosure and it was always taken, but you can never always know who has taken it.

The orphan cubs had been in the sett for only a week when I decided to replace the wire door with a wooden door with a small six-inch circular hole; this would allow the cubs to come out and, if there were problems, to run back in and, hopefully, the hole was too small for Bluebell to chase through after them. As soon as we fitted the door, one of the cubs, Thistle, came out and wandered into the chamber where Bluebell and her cubs were sleeping. Snuggling down, he was ready to go to sleep with them. I could not believe it was going to be that easy. All of a sudden it was realized there was a stranger in the camp and all hell was let loose. Thistle ran for his life, whipped through the small hole, back into the safety of the chamber shared with his mates! I was going to have to watch very carefully but no more happened during the day.

Carrying down a bucket of water later in the day, I looked into the sett and could hear a lot of commotion coming from the back tunnel where the young cubs were. Bluebell had got in there! Opening the back section, I shouted at her to come out. How she had managed to squeeze through that hole, I will never know, but she was very hot and panting from the effort. Pushing past all the cubs which were down the tunnel like a line of sausages, she waddled out. She knocked over the bucket of water, and lay on her back in the spilt water to cool herself down. She looked so funny stretched out like a panda.

I took all the doors away after that, and Bluebell took on all the cubs. On entering the chambers she would clean her two cubs and

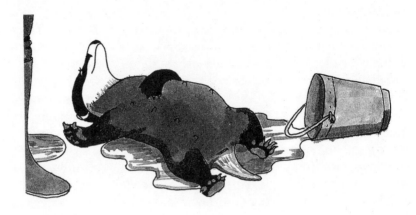

. . . she looked so funny stretched out like a panda.

then move on to the next chamber and clean the other three. The sight of all the cubs playing together and preening was amazing, and I am sure the visitors did not always realize just how privileged they were.

There were a few weeks during August when it was exceptionally hot and all the badgers moved into the tunnels, probably to be near the breeze by the opening. This meant that although there were six badgers at home, there was nothing on view – I wonder if they move nearer the surface in a similar way in the wild?

Although we deal with many animals, there are certain ones that are special to you. Snowdrop was one of these. She was a very tiny badger brought in to us as a road casualty, having been found unconscious on the side of the road. The birds had pecked one of her eyes out while she had lain there. She was thought to be only a cub. She was very dehydrated and in a state of collapse when she arrived and I took her straight through to Barry. Examination revealed that she had at one time been a lactating female so was older than a cub, but in her condition she could never have reared her cubs and they must have died. Placed on a drip, she was with the vet for three days, and then they felt she was well enough to have the eye removed properly before coming back to me.

When I brought her home, I placed her on a fresh straw bed in the care pen. She curled up in a tight ball, nose tucked into her body, and it was as if she had given up all will to live. I named her Snowdrop. She had such a tiny head with the clear black and white markings of a young badger, but her body was so tiny. Her scrawny legs showed how pitifully thin she was, the bones very evident with folds of skin hanging from her form. Her coat was dull and lifeless. She refused to eat or drink and eventually, in order to keep her alive, I was back to injecting fluids under the skin. Talking quietly to her as I tended her, I felt almost inclined to let her die, she seemed so unhappy. Sandra from the Wildlife Unit suggested that I tried her with Complan, honey and beaten egg so I mixed some up and slowly syringed it into her mouth. She liked the taste of that and swallowed it down. I did this six times a day; after a couple of days, she started to lift her head as I entered the pen. Slowly lowering the syringe, I eventually got her to lap from a dish and began to feel she was getting better. Gradually she began to put on weight. Her eye healed completely and she looked a lot better, but she rarely moved about and I could not get her to eat solids. Barry called in to see her as I was afraid that she might have some brain damage, but he still thought it best to continue a little bit longer. She was now beginning to look so much better: she had put on weight, her coat now had a shine to it and she took an interest in what you were doing, although she still did not move very far. For two months that badger was on Complan, honey and eggs – even by starving her, I could not get her on to solids.

September brought its lovely misty mornings and autumn shades. Time for the badger gate to be opened and for the cubs to face the world. The first night that freedom was offered, Bluebell came to see us at the house but the cubs were kept well away. Everyone returned the next morning, but definitely dirty from their explorations. They all piled on top of each other, the bottom ones struggling to the top every so often when it got too hot! Soon there were territorial paths appearing in the garden where they were taking their routine walks. My mother, who does a lot of watering in their neat garden by my parents' chalet in the back garden, was getting a lot of her plants uprooted. All those lovely worms and beetles that she was encouraging! Snuffle holes appeared on the lawn and a lot of activity behind the haybarn showed the excavation of a new sett. Even so all the badgers continued to return to the observation sett right through to November.

Snowdrop was still on her fluid diet, but as fat as butter, when I was offered another badger for a short while. Jojo had been knocked down near Cannington and had broken her front leg and displaced her hip. I wondered if she would be company for Snowdrop. When she arrived she was a very big sow badger, almost twice the size of the finely built Snowdrop. Jojo was already putting on her fat reserve for the winter and had quite a lot of weight behind her, so I hoped they were going to be all right. Certainly there was no problem in getting on with each other. To start with there was a wall of straw between their backs, which declared that they did not belong together, but after a few days they accepted each other and the wall disappeared. Whether or not it was the competition for food, Snowdrop started to eat solid food. It was two months before Jojo was well enough to return to her sett, and by this time a badger called Wheat was about to join us, again from the RSPCA, so this meant that once Jojo went, Snowdrop would not be on her own.

I had previously been out to where Jojo was found, to find the nearest sett for releasing her. Becky, the veterinary nurse at Colin Cheetham's surgery, came with me when we released her as she had answered the call to pick Jojo up and we wanted to make sure she went back to the same place. Becky is a very petite young lady with long hair, and is completely mad on animals – she has eight dogs herself, besides rats and mice (also a very understanding mother!). We commented on the fact that Jojo had been very quiet in the carrying case at the back of the car, but as soon as we arrived, lifted her out and put the case on the grass, she went frantic. She sensed she was home. When the front of the case was opened she came straight out, paused and looked at us, and was through the hedge and into the sett that she knew was there.

On the way home, Becky and I discussed the pleasures of looking after animals. She at that time was looking after a dog from the RSPCA dog and cat home. Becky explained that the bitch had been found in a deserted caravan and had since had four puppies. The mother was a poodle cross Yorkshire terrier and it was thought that the father was a Jack Russell, but each puppy was different and she had been unable to find homes for them. Needless to say, I swallowed the disguised offer hook, line and sinker, and returned home with a scruffy ragamuffin of a dog which we called Pollyanna (mainly after the Lunn Poly adverts on television, because Derek kept mimicking their catchphrase and telling her to 'get away'). Still, she's my little dog and an absolute poppet. Needless to say, due to her puppy habits she was nicknamed Piddly Polly!

From November onwards the numbers in the observation sett varied as the badgers started to spread out and move into setts around the farm. Occasionally we still catch them going through the yard, but they are totally wild and have never picked up the trust that Bluebell shows us.

The plan was to integrate Wheat and Snowdrop with Bluebell in the spring, as long as Bluebell did not have cubs again. Each morning I got into the habit of checking Bluebell and then the others in the care pen. As we drew nearer to the end of February, I began to think that Bluebell would not be having cubs in 1993. She had been on her own in the chambers for months, and I had wondered if this might be a sign of new arrivals, but it was not to be. Making sure all was well with Bluebell, I went on to look at Wheat and Snowdrop in the care pen. I was surprised to see that, instead of being curled up together, Wheat was down one end and Snowdrop was in some straw at the other end. I could see blood and my immediate reaction was that they had been fighting. It was not until looking closer that I could see two tiny badger cubs squirming around between Snowdrop's front paws. It had never occurred to me that she would have cubs, especially after being so ill. After all she had been through in the past year, it was wonderful to see her with her new family. She lifted her head and looked at me; although one eye is shut she still has such a pretty face and seemed so proud of her new cubs.

I have had the pleasure of seeing those cubs grow, of seeing Snowdrop's delight in her new family, a boy and a girl called Dusk and Dawn. It will be a success story when eventually they have their freedom, but in the meantime all the work that has gone into getting her as healthy and happy as she is now has been so worthwhile.

10

You Can Do It Too!

My parents met during the war when both of them were in the police force stationed at Gravesend. Dad volunteered to join the Royal Air Force and served as an observer (navigator bomb aimer). They married in 1941, and were parted for nearly three years whilst Dad was trained in South Africa and involved with secret raids in North Africa, Sicily and Italy. Only a third of his squadron survived the war. At the end of the war, Dad continued his career in the police force. My sister, June, was born in 1946 and I followed in 1950. (I can see you all calculating my age!)

Due to Dad's work, we moved several times in Kent and learnt to adjust to new surroundings and friends at various times throughout our lives. It was a very happy childhood with domestic animals always being part of it. We always had dogs, and the menagerie grew over the years to include rabbits, guinea-pigs, budgies and canaries, hamsters – not forgetting the proverbial goldfish. I can remember that Dad was always the one who took the dogs for the early morning walk and, if it had been raining, we two girls had to dry the dogs' feet when they got home. We were taught to respect animals, and people as well; they all have a place in the world and one should never expect them always to do what you want them to do!

Mum was the one with the patience if anything was ever ill,

and we all enjoyed the fun when Susie, our corgi, was allowed to have a litter of pups. My sarcasm and humour has been inherited from my father – he was well known for it in the force. I love the story that he tells of when he was still a young PC on night duty patrolling the Gravesend Docks. It was the early hours of a cold November morning as he walked up towards the end of the moorings. The water was lapping quietly as the tide began to turn and all that could be heard was the constant throbbing of the industrial machinery that was on the go, day and night. Suddenly the sound of a man running echoed down the dark riverside and the outline of a middle-aged man frantically making his way towards him became clearer. My father stood quietly assessing the situation as the man reached him, sweat pouring from his face from the effort of running, yet completely drained of colour.

'Can I help you, sir?' asked my father quietly.

Leaning against the lamppost, the man bent over, trying to regain his breath. Hysterically he gasped. 'I've found a body, I've found a body.'

'And exactly where, sir, is this body?' questioned my father.

'Over there,' the poor man sobbed, 'on the side of the river.'

Trying to defuse the situation, my father replied: 'Don't worry, sir. We shall take it back to the station, place it in Found Property, and if after three weeks nobody has claimed it – it's yours!'

Sometimes we lived in towns, but mostly we were lucky and lived in the country; but wherever we were, we were always able to find places to walk the dogs, so the pleasure of walking through fields and woods has been with me from an early age – whether it is a family outing, a walk with friends, or a time for being alone, just me and the dogs. However, I was never aware of the creatures that lived there, apart from the fleeting glimpse of a fox or rabbit.

My mother originated from Kingston upon Thames, but my father was a true Londoner. Although they liked the rural areas, they had no real knowledge of wildlife ecology or farming. (My father always says that the only farming he has ever done was farming out the work to others in his Division!) It must have been a surprise to them both when June and I left school to become dairymaids. My father, then an Inspector, retired from the police force in 1965 and moved to Somerset, where he took up an appointment as Managing Clerk to the Clerk of the Peace for Bristol. June by then was working on a farm in Smarden in Kent, so she stayed behind; she has since married and still lives there with her three horses, two donkeys and four dogs.

My first job was working on a farm in Gloucestershire as a dairymaid at Pennywell Farm. There was a herd of Guernsey and Jersey cows and also poultry houses. At that time the cows were milked in a cowshed. They all entered the stall and had chains put round their necks, and it was my job to go along and wash the udders ready for the farmer to come behind and put the milking clusters on. My parents, when visiting me a month later, came with me when I brought the cows in for milking. As I called them by the gate, the cows all started to make their way towards us. Pointing to different cows, Mum and Dad asked their names and were amused that I could not tell them until they had walked past us and their rear end was in view. I was so used to seeing the back end, whilst they were in the stalls, that this was the way I recognized them. It took a few more months before I began to know their faces!

From there, my life has been varied, changing from farming to hotel and catering, before eventually coming back to Somerset to settle here. Chance has given me the opportunity of helping wildlife and the more I do, the more I realize the importance of knowing about the animal itself, its habitat and territory. There is no point in spending hours, days, even months in returning an animal or bird to full health if you are just going to let it go, with no thought as to how it will survive once released. Warning bells should ring if you are told that a nocturnal animal is 'out in the day, playing in the sunshine' and vice versa: you need to know your animals.

Maybe you do not want to become involved, but there are still many things that can be done to help wildlife without too much involvement at all. Litter must be one of the important things. Discarded bottles and cans become lethal traps to small mammals. Out of curiosity, the tiny animal will enter a can lying at an angle but will be unable to get out because of the slippery surface. It is estimated that 15 million small mammals die each year in this way. Discarded food tins get trapped on the heads of hedgehogs and the legs of foxes, badgers and deer. Even the plastic surrounds that hold four beer cans together are lethal when caught round the body of hedgehogs and seagulls.

It may not be your rubbish, but it is still a danger to wildlife. If we were all prepared to pick up this and that, which we find left lying around, things would soon improve. It's one thing to tut-tut and complain about it, but just how many of us are prepared to *do* something about it?

Hedgehogs especially are not incredibly intelligent, and they are often the casualties even in our own gardens. If you have a pond, make sure that one side is sloping to allow a hedgehog to scrabble out after an unexpected swim, and keeping the pond topped up will make getting a drink easier and so reduce the risk of a hedgehog falling in. Hedgehogs can easily get tangled in netting placed in vegetable gardens for runner beans, and of course that bonfire looks really quite inviting to make a nest in. If you must create a bonfire, start the fire beside the pile and move the rubbish over as it burns; that way you might find residents before it is too late! Cattle grids are also a particular trap for hedgehogs, but it is quite easy to build a small ramp inside, to allow any unfortunates to climb back out.

Development of residential areas is on the increase because of the need for new homes, and many animals have adapted to living in urban areas, especially the fox and, to an extent, the badger as well. We have managed to protect the badger sett through legislation, but what is the point if we build right up to his doorstep and take away his foraging area? A home is no good without a food supply.

By creating gardens that encourage insect life, birds and mammals will follow. Try not to be too tidy. If you are a hedgehog, you are looking for a garden with a food supply of slugs and insects, places to build nests and building material of twigs and leaves. Allow an area to grow wild to offer seeds and berries to the birds which can be a source of delight throughout the year as you watch them come and feed. You will be repaid in full by the variety of birds that will visit your garden.

There are many societies and groups that you can belong to who will advise you and offer you the chance to learn a great deal more about specific subjects. I have listed several of these at the back of the book. The Royal Society for Nature Conservation will tell you of conservation groups within your area. We are very lucky here to have the Somerset Trust for Nature Conservation, which is a very active society with many extremely knowledgeable members. There is a year-round programme of events including walks, films, talks, exhibitions and social evenings. They also manage nature reserves, over sixty in Somerset totalling 3,000 acres, and volunteers are always needed to help with the practical work, which is a chance to work alongside experts and gain experience in this way. There are also specialist groups within the society for badgers, bats, invertebrates, butterflies, moths, plants and geology, as well as a junior club to encourage our children to know more about the world we live in. This is certainly one way of becoming more involved with wildlife in your area.

Bristol University offers various courses on British wildlife, and even on occasions has Wildlife Care Courses for which you can enrol. We now have a British Wildlife Rehabilitation Council which has recently been formed in the effort to consolidate the work being carried out throughout the country by dedicated people prepared to help wildlife on a voluntary basis. The idea is to build up a record system of casualties and to pass on information and data gained from other people's experience in this field of work, of which there is as yet little knowledge.

I have been very lucky to have the RSPCA's Wildlife Unit at West Hatch near to me, and over the years I have come to know Colin and Sandra, who run the unit. They have always been prepared to advise on problems that I have had, and it really does help to have someone to talk things through with at times. There is another RSPCA Wildlife Unit in Norfolk, besides many other groups throughout the country, who are only too happy to pass on information to help people prepared to carry out work involving wildlife. All these groups are usually looking for volunteers in one way or another and by finding out about them, usually through your local library, you can then approach them if you have time to offer.

There are occasions when I have heard criticism of the RSPCA, maybe for not responding or not even being interested. Often this is because, unfortunately, the telephone call is answered by one of the most hated inventions – the answerphone. (How many of us have been told 'I have rung loads of times, but each time all I get is that wretched answering machine'? – Um, would it perhaps be a good idea to leave a message?) I'm afraid the RSPCA is no different from most businesses, and manpower must be used efficiently. It is better to have that person out working and then returning to messages at certain times, than to have someone sitting waiting for the phone to ring. They are also very stretched with Inspectors having to cover large areas, which can sometimes cause delay in actioning a call. This is where specialist groups often come in useful, and the badger groups particularly are often asked by the RSPCA to take on call-outs that involve badgers.

Public awareness is increasing and at times, particularly in the spring and early summer when there are young animals around, calls to the RSPCA increase tremendously. Known people with the correct facilities and expertise will be asked to support them. Yes, they make mistakes but then I certainly could not put my hand on my heart and say that I had never made one, nor probably could many others if they were honest. If we make a mistake, the important thing is to learn from it, find out what should have been done and do the utmost to make sure that the mistake does not happen again.

One experience we had, which luckily had a happy ending, was soon after we were open to the public. We had many different kinds of poultry and very often would sit the hens on fertile eggs which duly hatched. The hen is usually a good mother and will keep the chicks tucked under her body to keep them warm. Simon, our son, was letting the bantams out one morning and found that a chick had fallen over the side of the box where the mother was sitting and had apparently died from the cold. Picking it up, he called to Derek who had just finished the morning milking and was making his way back to the house for breakfast. Derek looked at the chick and, placing it in the empty corn bucket, told Simon to check that the other chicks were all right and then come on up for breakfast – he was not to worry about it, these things happen.

Having checked the other chicks, which were fine, Simon leapt over the fence and ran to catch Derek up.

'Shall I throw it in for the ferrets to eat?' asked Simon – ever the sadistic one of the family (our chief tick-remover!).

'No,' said Derek, restraining him, 'You're not really sure why it died and if it has got anything wrong with it, it could make the ferrets ill. Put it on the Rayburn.' (I'm afraid that we dispose of most of our small bodies in this way, seeing as it is the cleanest method. We find that if animals or birds are buried, they merely get dug up again by either fox or badger. When animals were ill, they would be placed by the slow oven of the Rayburn for warmth and warned that, if they did not get better, they would end up in the fire side of the Rayburn – they usually got better!)

I had just riddled the Rayburn and filled it with stove nuts while breakfast was cooking, when I heard them arriving in the backhouse. Simon, in his usual way, rushed in to tell me the bad news and threw the chick in the Rayburn. Both the men washed their hands and I got the drinks ready. Derek was saying what a shame it was to have lost the chick, especially as the hen had only hatched five chicks in the first place.

Opening the papers, we sat round the table and started our breakfast. Silence fell as we began to eat. Suddenly a plaintive cheeping could be heard, and we all looked at each other wondering where it was coming from. To our horror we realized it was coming from the Rayburn. Dashing to the fire door, Derek opened it wide and there stood a very sooty chick which had warmed through quite nicely now and was fully revived. Being freshly filled with fuel, the fire had only just started to burn through and so far the chick had not got hot feet, but I hate to think what could have happened if the Rayburn had not been freshly filled!

So – point number one must be to make sure it is dead. Poultry chicks are notorious for appearing dead when chilled, so it is best to give them the benefit of the doubt and provide them with some heat before giving up on them completely. Remember that animals that

. . . there stood a very sooty chick . . .

hibernate will also give the appearance of being dead, so either use a mirror to check their breathing or invest in a cheap stethoscope which you can usually buy from a vet for around £5.

Badgers, in particular, are one animal that can withstand tremendous impact in an accident and it has been found that a large number of badgers assumed to be dead on the side of the road are sometimes just unconscious and in shock, and will often respond to treatment. Badger group members are often asked to check these casualties if it is at all possible, though obviously never putting themselves at risk.

If you find an injured animal, the first important thing to do is to cover it, using either a blanket or an item of clothing if nothing else is to hand. Once covered, you have reduced the stress that the debilitated animal is suffering. If it is a large animal, such as a deer, you can cover just the head. A pillowcase or cloth money bag with a corner cut out for the nose is ideal. If the animal has some mobility, it is important to contain it in some way.

When you come upon a problem, take time to assess the situation. Keep away from the animal or bird, so as not to frighten it, and work out the routes of escape that may be available to the casualty and how you can feasibly block them off. Believe you me, there is nothing more disheartening than to see a mortally wounded animal escape and know that it is going to endure a lingering death. Better to wait for an extra pair of hands than to attempt heroics that could prove unsuccessful.

It could be that you do not wish to take on the responsibility of transporting the casualty to a vet. If not, then once it is covered or contained in a box (again covered so that the animal cannot see out), contact the RSPCA or a known animal centre, a local veterinary surgeon or, if all else fails, the police.

Let us say that you have decided to take on the responsibility for the problem. Often it will be a road casualty, as unfortunately these form a high percentage of all injuries incurred. Find a container in which to put the casualty; it may be unconscious, but that is not to say that it will not come round in a warm vehicle as you make your way home. Remember that any animal that has teeth can and will bite if frightened and cornered. They are not to know that you are trying to help, and will usually resist in any way that they can unless too ill to do so. Also, be very careful in the way that you lift them in case of back injuries.

It is unlikely that a vet will be able to see you immediately, so if you are not far from home, it is better to get the casualty home and place it somewhere warm, quiet and dark. Warmth is crucial. Remember that you think you are helping the creature, but everything that you are doing is alien to the casualty. Being put in a car is in itself a terrifying thing, so think about the animal. Don't put the radio on (or the tape), and keep the container away from dogs. Better to be put in the boot than to have a hairy adversary sniffing around the box. Make movements slowly and positively and talk softly to the animal. I am sure it will pick up the tenderness in your voice. First aid for animals is the same as for humans, so first of all, don't panic. Unless there is bleeding to stem, the casualty is best left alone. Try to resist looking at it too often.

Your next step is to find a vet who is prepared to accept wild animals. This is not always easy, but once you find the right vet you are in luck. This really is important – you are only as good as your vet is. We have been so lucky with Colin Cheetham and Barry Parsons for all that they have done for us and for their infinite care. The right vet will attend wildlife, usually only charging for materials used, and will also impart knowledge to you so that the next time you will feel more experienced; eventually you will start to cope with simple situations that are within your scope. It will take time, and knowledge will come from guidance from your vet and from practice as each problem arises. You cannot become a qualified vet just by reading books; if you undertake something that you do not yet have the expertise to carry out, you can cause more pain and suffering than you are trying to relieve.

If a vet is not immediately available, the only thing that is important to do is make water available to the casualty, and preferably lectades which contain extra minerals to start them on the right road to recovery. If you can obtain liquid lectade from your vet or local farm supplier, it is easier to dilute small quantities.

To summarize, the four most important things are: (1) warmth; (2) quiet; (3) water; (4) darkness.

My bible is the book *Care of the Wild* by W. J. Jordan and John Hughes. I find it easy to use and of great value. You look up the animal concerned and then everything you need to know is clearly explained, from capture to feeding and eventual release. It is also a book suitable just to read; the address it is available from is given at the back of this book. The only thing I would say is that very many

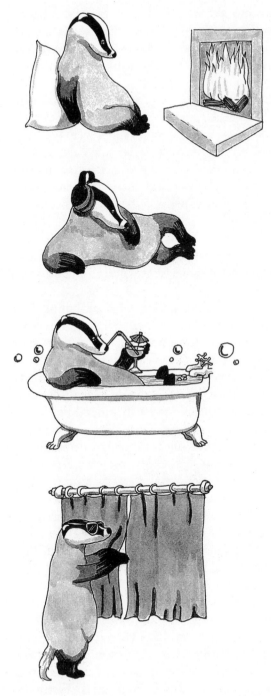

1. *Warmth* 2. *Quiet* 3. *Water* 4. *Darkness*

milk substitutes have been produced since the book was written, and there are now many different and better brands that can be used other than the ones mentioned in the book. Of course there are many other books written on this subject, but this one I find easiest to follow.

Birds die from shock, so they are treated differently from mammals. They really are best left for several hours before trying to do anything, or even contacting a vet. As long as water is available to them, they are best left. If they survive that interim period, then is the time to think of a trip to the vet.

Certain animals require licences if they are protected species. Daytime birds of prey must only be held by licensed rehabilitators or registered keepers. Badgers, dormice, grey squirrel, mink and bats require licences. That is not to say that they cannot be picked up for welfare purposes, but English Nature must be notified that they are in your possession (you will find their address at the back of this book).

Do not be too quick in taking birds and animals in. Sometimes we act too fast, particularly where fledglings are concerned. When fully fledged they leave the nest but the parents continue to feed them, finding them by their plaintive calls which we sometimes misconstrue as calls for help. By this time the bird has learnt to fear humans and it is highly unlikely that, if taken into captivity, they will ever feed. Unless danger is impending, they really are best left alone.

Badger cubs, fox cubs and often baby deer are picked up when often mum is not far away. If you see anything young, don't immediately pick it up – stand away and watch. Usually they know the way home, or mum is nearby. It is only necessary to take action if they are visibly stressed, shaking and crying. Indeed, if the mother is known to have been killed but the young are weaned, it may be possible to feed them near their sett or earth rather than take them into captivity. At least then they will have a familiar territory to live in.

I do not intend to advise on treatment as I truly believe this must be given with guidance, but I hope that some of you will go on to become more involved in helping our wildlife. If you become as busy as we are, you will begin to realize the importance of record-keeping and of certain procedures that are essential – for example, how it is better to keep cages containing predators away from animals that would be their food – unsettling for both parties! Animal welfare centres will give you advice willingly.

You will also find out that not only are you treating the animals themselves but also the people that bring the casualties in. They are usually upset from finding them, or have even been partly to blame for what has happened to the creature. They themselves feel happier if they have taken them to someone who cares, and are usually grateful if you can spare the time to let them know the outcome, even if the animal dies.

As I have said before, you will not always do things right. I had a telephone call at 10 o'clock one evening from a lady. She explained that earlier in the day she and her husband had tried to move a duck with a brood of freshly hatched ducklings out of her neighbour's garden, away from the danger of their dog. The duck had misconstrued their intentions and, faced with this danger, had decided to fly off and leave the young to cope for themselves. Upset that their actions had caused the mother to desert, they had rounded up the seven ducklings, placed them in a box and put them in the front room. They had rigged up a microphone by the box and, using an amplifier, were relaying their calls into the garden in the hope that the mother would return. So far she hadn't; did I think she would?

Suppressing the thought that this was a wind-up, I advised that as by now it was nearly dark, it was highly unlikely that she would return, so the best thing to do was to keep them warm.

'Did they drink milk?' I was asked, and again I tried to keep my voice level as the mental picture arose of a duck with twelve teats hanging down. I explained that they didn't, but that the ducklings could be fed on biscuit crumbs until the morning and then, if the lady and her husband came out to the farm, I would give the ducklings some proper food. But they must keep them warm – about 80 degrees. Yes, that was no problem.

Early the next morning a car drove into the yard, with two very seriously faced people. They had under-estimated how warm the ducklings needed to be and sadly only two had survived the night. I told them not to blame themselves as the shock of being caught and losing their mother would all take its toll. Peering into the box that they offered me. I could see one duckling that seemed all right but the other had its head twisted and did not look too good. We went over to the poultry room; there I had a hen who had been sitting on some eggs but they were no good, so I wondered if she would take to these ducklings. Normally I would do this at night, but I tried it anyway: quietly holding a duckling in my hand, I slid my hand under the hen, left the duckling behind, and took out an egg. We stood back and watched.

The hen was a large white Sussex hen, and she cocked her head on one side as the cheeping sounded from under her ruffled skirt. She quietly tidied the straw around her nest and again cocked her head on one side. She decided to put her head under her body to have a sort round, and, finding a duckling which she had no intention of taking to, hoisted it out of the nest with a fling of disgust. The woman standing behind me squealed that she had killed it, but it was all right, just sitting bewildered on the edge of the pen.

I could see that this wasn't going to work so, retrieving the duckling, I decided to put the two in a lighted box which we have for tiny chicks. It is just a square box with a glass front and a lid with a light attachment, with the light bulb creating enough heat for the chicks. I placed the ducklings in the box, and they settled in the warm shavings. The husband, looking at the box, decided that he could build a box like that and then they could take the ducklings back and rear them at home.

I said that this was a good idea, but that they should now go away and wait until 11 o'clock, then ring to see if the ducklings were still alive, as shock so easily kills tiny things. If they were alive by then, they could go ahead with their plan and come back and collect them.

The car disappeared out of the yard and I went to get small dishes for water and food to go in the box. Returning to the poultry room, I was disappointed to see that the sickly duckling had died and was on its back with its legs in the air. I was cross with myself that I had not emphasized the need for warmth. As I took the body out, the other duckling dabbled in the water and preened. Hopefully, at least they would have one to look after. I disposed of the dead duckling in the Rayburn.

An hour later, I returned to the poultry room to check on the progress of the other duckling. To my horror, it was dead. Switching the lamp off, I again disposed of the body in the Rayburn and went to the office. I left instructions that when the couple rang at 11 o'clock, the office staff were to call me so that I could explain the situation. They didn't ring.

Just after lunch the couple returned, the man triumphant that he had finished the box for the ducklings. With a heavy heart I went to meet them and told them that both ducklings had unfortunately died, and how very sorry I was as the couple were both very upset. This, I explained, was why I asked them to ring at 11 o'clock, in case the shock had taken its toll.

Close to tears, the man explained that he had made a small coffin for the five ducklings that had died previously, so that he could bury them in the garden near where they had hatched. My heart churned as he asked if he could have the bodies back of the other two that had died so that they could be placed in the coffin with the others. As gently as I could, I explained that we had incinerated them in the Rayburn as this was the cleanest method of disposing of bodies. They were both horrified at the thought and, despite my profuse apologies, left with no intentions of ever coming back again.

Later that afternoon, a local person phoned to say he had an injured blackbird in his garden and could I look after it? He was told to bring it in. Striding into the farm a while later, the man, complete with cardboard box, came to give me his casualty.

'If it gets better,' he asked, 'could I have it back to put in the garden?'

'Yes, sure,' I replied. 'But if it dies – do you want the body back?'

He laughed and said, no, he didn't really think so. Good, I explained, because I've already done it wrong once today and I'm not going to do it again! Rule number 2 – don't get rid of the body until you are sure it is not wanted.

There will be many times when things will die on you. The RSPCA, even with all their expertise, only expect a 50 per cent success rate. This is something you must learn to expect. It is also important that you follow your own beliefs. There is nothing worse than doing something that you have been told is the best thing to do, when you have a gut feeling that you want to do something else. At the end of the day, you are the person who will have to accept the responsibility if a creature dies and it is no good for your confidence if are you going to wish that you had followed your own instincts. Remember, too, that animals are all individuals – maybe Mrs Smith's badger cubs did eat scrambled eggs, when yours will only eat weetabix, but that's not important – what is important is that they *are* eating.

Ethics are an important issue and these again are something that only you can come to terms with. My own personal view is that the aim of all care is for the return of that creature to the wild, and if, through disability, this is not possible then euthanasia becomes an option. Only on rare occasions, when animals will accept the restriction of life in captivity and yet still have quality of life, do I think that, for educational purposes, it is fair to keep an animal that can never be released. This, as I say, is something only you can decide; it is up to your conscience.

Don't be afraid to have a go. 'What if it dies?' I hear you say. Well, if you do not take any action and the animal is injured or orphaned, it is going to die anyway. Remember that by the time a wild animal shows symptoms and allows itself to be caught, it is usually very ill indeed, so there will be failures. But when you have the joy of nursing an animal to full health and seeing it eventually returning to its home, it will all seem worthwhile.

We have almost become victims of our own success. The work with the wildlife increases as we become better known, and so do the costs! Strain on the finances and facilities led us in 1992 to look to other people for support, and the Bluebell Sett was founded. This offers membership as 'friends of the farm' to help finance the welfare work that we do. A committee runs the group entirely separately from the farm, and Simon King, the well-known film-maker, is the patron of the group. We thought it would be nice to name the group after Bluebell the badger, especially as in 1992, as well as having two cubs of her own, she adopted three orphaned cubs and so is doing her fair share of the work!

So remember, it can cost money, but if you have decided to become involved – the best of luck.

I have led a very charmed life, where wonderful opportunities have come my way. Even being able to write this book has given me the chance to share with you the joys and sorrows of working with animals. Thank goodness for an understanding husband and family, for there are times when it involves a lot of work, but the unique chance of being so close to such wild and beautiful creatures has entirely been my privilege.

Further Reading

Care of the Wild by W. J. Jordan and John Hughes
First aid and care for wild animals.
Available from:
Care for the Wild,
1 Ashfolds,
Horsham Road,
Rusper,
West Sussex RH12 4QX
Tel: 0293 871596

Hedgehogs by Pat Morris and *Badgers* by Michael Clark
Both available from:
Whittet Books Ltd,
18 Anley Road,
London W14 OBY

Natural History of Badgers by Ernest Neal
Croom Helm Ltd,
Provident House,
Burrell Row,
Beckenham,
Kent BR3 1AT

The Country Life Guide to Artificial Badger Setts by Penny
Cresswell, Warren Cresswell and Michael Woods
For information on artificial setts.
Available from:
Country Life Badger Booklet,
7 London Road,
Tetbury,
Gloucestershire GL8 8JQ

Useful Addresses

Royal Society for the Prevention of Cruelty to Animals Wildlife Centres:

RSPCA Wildlife Field Unit,
West Hatch,
Taunton,
Somerset TA3 5RT

Tel: 01823 480156

RSPCA Norfolk Wildlife Hospital,
East Winch,
Norfolk PE32 1NR

Tel: 01553 840045

British Wildlife Rehabilitation Council, for details of Wildlife Rescue Centres or in order to receive the BRWC Newsletter write to:

Mr Tim Thomas,
RSPCA Wildlife Department,
Causeway,
Horsham,
West Sussex RH12 1HG

Care for the Wild,
Worldwide Animal Rescue,
1, Ashfolds,
Horsham Road,
Rusper,
West Sussex,
RH12 4QX

(Animal Sponsorship)

Societies

Royal Society for the Prevention of Cruelty to Animals,
Causeway,
Horsham,
West Sussex,
RH12 1HG

(Adult and Child membership)

Royal Society for Nature Conservation,
The Green,
Witham Park,
Lincoln,
LN5 7JR

Somerset Wildlife Trust
Fyne Court,
Broomfield,
Bridgwater,
Somerset,
TA5 2EQ
Tel: 01823 451587

(Child and Adult Membership)

Royal Society for the Protection of Birds,
The Lodge,
Sandy,
Bedfordshire,
SG19 2DL

National Federation of Badger Groups,
15, Cloisters Business Centre,
8, Battersea Park Road,
London,
SW8 4BG

English Nature,
Northminster House,
Peterborough,
Cambridgeshire,
PE1 1UA

Mammal Society,
Cloisters House,
Cloisters Business Centre,
8, Battersea Park Road,
London,
SW8 4BG

The Fox Project,
P.O. Box 56,
Tonbridge,
Kent,
TN9 1XY

The Hedgehog Preservation Society,
Knowbury House,
Ludlow,
Shropshire,
SY8 3LQ

Hedgehog Helpline,
Kay Heaton-Jones,
5, Foreland Road,
Whitchurch,
Cardiff.

Wildlife Courses,
University of Bristol,
Department for Continuing Education,
Wills Memorial Building,
Queens Road,
Bristol,
BS8 1HR

British Chelonian Group,
P.O. Box 235,
Lincoln,
LN6 8AX

Bluebell Sett Wildlife Appeal

We are desperately seeking friends of the farm who will support, through membership of Bluebell Sett, the wildlife work that is carried out at this farm.

Over the years our reputation for taking orphaned and injured animals has grown, many cases being referred to us by vets and the RSPCA as well as members of the public. We have gained experience with all kinds of animals and improved our facilities so that much of the work can be carried out behind the scenes thus aiding recovery by reducing the stress induced by human presence. We have a hospital room with heat lamps, and larger pens to take foxes and badgers that have been injured, usually in road accidents.

Our main aim is to get the animals fit and healthy and then return them to the wild. They are either released where they were found or, if more suitable, from here. Some are taken to the RSPCA Wildlife Unit at Hatch Beauchamp with whom we work very closely.

Over a thousand wild animals have been treated since 1986 when we first started to care for the wild. We never send animals away and are available 24 hours a day – but it is all time-consuming and intensive work. Our vets bill alone is nearly £2000 a year and, like most businesses today we are having to deal with cashflow problems. The bank has now told us that they can no longer support this side of the business which shows no financial return. We feel, however, that the work we do is too important to abandon without trying to raise some support. An annual amount of £5000 is needed.

We are also involved in the National Breeding Programme for the Common Dormouse. Despite the name these delightful creatures are now quite rare and it is hoped to be able to re-introduce them into woodland areas where they have already become extinct.

WOULD YOU LIKE TO JOIN THE BLUEBELL SETT?

Members receive a pack containing a certificate of membership, a car sticker, admission discount vouchers, animal factsheets and a letter from Simon King. The presentation is such that this makes an ideal Christmas or birthday gift. Subscriptions are: adults £12.50, children £7.00; family £30; concessions (OAP and unemployed) £8.50. Please contact Pauline Kidner at Secret World, East Huntspill, Somerset, TA9 3PZ for further details.